MznLnx

Missing Links Exam Preps

Exam Prep for

Futures, Options, and Swaps

Kolb, 4th Edition

The MznLnx Exam Prep is your link from the textbook and lecture to your exams. The MznLnx Exam Preps are unauthorized and comprehensive reviews of your textbooks.

All material provided by MznLnx and Rico Publications (c) 2010
Textbook publishers and textbook authors do not particpate in or contribute to these reviews.

MznLnx

Rico
Publications

Exam Prep for Futures, Options, and Swaps
4th Edition
Kolb

Publisher: Raymond Houge
Assistant Editor: Michael Rouger
Text and Cover Designer: Lisa Buckner
Marketing Manager: Sara Swagger
Project Manager, Editorial Production: Jerry Emerson
Art Director: Vernon Lowerui

Product Manager: Dave Mason
Editorial Assitant: Rachel Guzmanji
Pedagogy: Debra Long
Cover Image: Jim Reed/Getty Images
Text and Cover Printer: City Printing, Inc.
Compositor: Media Mix, Inc.

(c) 2010 Rico Publications
ALL RIGHTS RESERVED. No part of this work covered by the copyright may be reproduced or used in any form or by an means--graphic, electronic, or mechanical, including photocopying, recording, taping, Web distribution, information storage, and retrieval systems, or in any other manner--without the written permission of the publisher.

Printed in the United States
ISBN:

For more information about our products, contact us at:

Dave.Mason@RicoPublications.com

For permission to use material from this text or product, submit a request online to:

Dave.Mason@RicoPublications.com

Contents

CHAPTER 1
Introduction ... 1

CHAPTER 2
Futures Markets ... 6

CHAPTER 3
Futures Prices ... 13

CHAPTER 4
Using Futures Markets ... 21

CHAPTER 5
Interest Rate Futures: Introduction ... 25

CHAPTER 6
Interest Rate Futures: Refinements ... 31

CHAPTER 7
Stock Index Futures: Introduction ... 36

CHAPTER 8
Stock Index Futures: Refinements ... 40

CHAPTER 9
Foreign Currency Futures ... 44

CHAPTER 10
The Options Market ... 48

CHAPTER 11
Option Payoffs and Option Strategies ... 53

CHAPTER 12
Bounds on Option Prices ... 58

CHAPTER 13
European Option Pricing ... 61

CHAPTER 14
Option Sensitivities and Option Hedging ... 65

CHAPTER 15
American Option Pricing ... 68

CHAPTER 16
Options on Stock Indexes, Foreign Currency, and Futures ... 69

CHAPTER 17
The Options Approach to Corporate Securities ... 71

CHAPTER 18
Exotic Options ... 75

CHAPTER 19
Interest Rate Options ... 77

CHAPTER 20
The Swaps Market: Introduction ... 85

Contents (Cont.)

CHAPTER 21   90
  Swaps: Economic Analysis and Pricing
CHAPTER 22   96
  Swaps: Applications
ANSWER KEY   102

TO THE STUDENT

COMPREHENSIVE

The *MznLnx* Exam Prep series is designed to help you pass your exams. Editors at MznLnx review your textbooks and then prepare these practice exams to help you master the textbook material. Unlike study guides, workbooks, and practice tests provided by the texbook publisher and textbook authors, *MznLnx* gives you **all** of the material in each chapter in exam form, not just samples, so you can be sure to nail your exam.

MECHANICAL

The MznLnx Exam Prep series creates exams that will help you learn the subject matter as well as test you on your understanding. Each question is designed to help you master the concept. Just working through the exams, you gain an understanding of the subject--its a simple mechanical process that produces success.

INTEGRATED STUDY GUIDE AND REVIEW

MznLnx is not just a set of exams designed to test you, its also a comprehensive review of the subject content. Each exam question is also a review of the concept, making sure that you will get the answer correct without having to go to other sources of material. You learn as you go! Its the easiest way to pass an exam.

HUMOR

Studying can be tedious and dry. MznLnx's instructional design includes moderate humor within the exam questions on occassion, to break the tedium and revitalize the brain

Chapter 1. Introduction

1. A _____ is a financial contract whose value is derived from the value of something else (known as the underlying.) The underlying on which a _____ is based can be an asset, weather conditions bonds or other forms of credit.
   a. 7-Eleven
   b. 4-4-5 Calendar
   c. 529 plan
   d. Derivative

2. A _____ is an agreement between two parties to buy or sell an asset at a specified point of time in the future. The price of the underlying instrument, in whatever form, is paid before control of the instrument changes. This is one of the many forms of buy/sell orders where the time of trade is not the time where the securities themselves are exchanged.
   a. Forward contract
   b. Loan Credit Default Swap Index
   c. Derivatives markets
   d. Constant maturity credit default swap

3. A _____ is an exchange of promises between two or more parties to do an act which is enforceable in a court of law. It is where an unqualified offer meets a qualified acceptance and the parties reach Consensus ad Idem. The parties must have the necessary capacity to _____ and the _____ must not be either trifling, indeterminate, impossible or illegal.
   a. 7-Eleven
   b. 529 plan
   c. Contract
   d. 4-4-5 Calendar

4. In banking and finance, _____ denotes all activities from the time a commitment is made for a transaction until it is settled. _____ is necessary because the speed of trades is much faster than the cycle time for completing the underlying transaction.

   In its widest sense _____ involves the management of post-trading, pre-settlement credit exposures, to ensure that trades are settled in accordance with market rules, even if a buyer or seller should become insolvent prior to settlement.
   a. Clearing house
   b. Procter ' Gamble
   c. Share
   d. Clearing

Chapter 1. Introduction

5. A _____ is a financial services company that provides clearing and settlement services for financial transactions, usually on a futures exchange, and often acts as central counterparty (the payor actually pays the _____, which then pays the payee). A _____ may also offer novation, the substitution of a new contract or debt for an old, or other credit enhancement services to its members.

The term is also used for banks like Suffolk Bank that acted as a restraint on the over-issuance of private bank notes.

    a. Bucket shop
    b. Warrant
    c. Clearing house
    d. Valuation

6. In finance, a _____ is a standardized contract, to buy or sell a specified commodity of standardized quality at a certain date in the future, at a market determined price (the futures price.)

The price is determined by the instantaneous equilibrium between the forces of supply and demand among competing buy and sell orders on the exchange at the time of the purchase or sale of the contract.

In many cases, the items may be such non-traditional 'commodities' as foreign currencies, commercial or government paper [e.g., bonds], or 'baskets' of corporate equity ['stock indices'] or other financial instruments.

    a. Financial future
    b. Heston model
    c. Repurchase agreement
    d. Futures contract

7. In finance, a _____ is collateral that the holder of a position in securities, options, or futures contracts has to deposit to cover the credit risk of his counterparty (most often his broker.) This risk can arise if the holder has done any of the following:

- borrowed cash from the counterparty to buy securities or options,
- sold securities or options short, or
- entered into a futures contract.

The collateral can be in the form of cash or securities, and it is deposited in a _____ account. On U.S. futures exchanges, '_____' was formally called performance bond.

_____ buying is buying securities with cash borrowed from a broker, using other securities as collateral.

Chapter 1. Introduction

a. Share
b. Procter ' Gamble
c. Credit
d. Margin

8. An _____ is a contract written by a seller that conveys to the buyer the right -- but not the obligation -- to buy (in the case of a call _____) or to sell (in the case of a put _____) a particular asset, such as a piece of property such as, among others, a futures contract. In return for granting the _____, the seller collects a payment (the premium) from the buyer.

For example, buying a call _____ provides the right to buy a specified quantity of a security at a set strike price at some time on or before expiration, while buying a put _____ provides the right to sell.

a. Annuity
b. Option
c. Amortization
d. AT'T Mobility LLC

9. A _____ is a financial contract between two parties, the buyer and the seller of this type of option. Often it is simply labeled a 'call'. The buyer of the option has the right, but not the obligation to buy an agreed quantity of a particular commodity or financial instrument (the underlying instrument) from the seller of the option at a certain time (the expiration date) for a certain price (the strike price.)

a. Bear spread
b. Bull spread
c. Bear call spread
d. Call option

10. A _____ is a financial contract between two parties, the seller (writer) and the buyer of the option. The put allows its buyer the right but not the obligation to sell a commodity or financial instrument (the underlying instrument) to the writer (seller) of the option at a certain time for a certain price (the strike price.) The writer (seller) has the obligation to purchase the underlying asset at that strike price, if the buyer exercises the option.

a. Put option
b. Bear call spread
c. Debit spread
d. Bear spread

Chapter 1. Introduction

11. A _____ is a foreign exchange agreement between two parties to exchange principal and fixed rate interest payments on a loan in one currency for principal and fixed rate interest payments on an equal (regarding net present value) loan in another currency. They are motivated by comparative advantage.

    a. Foreign exchange market
    b. Currency pair
    c. Forex swap
    d. Currency swap

12. _____ is a fee paid on borrowed assets. It is the price paid for the use of borrowed money, or, money earned by deposited funds. Assets that are sometimes lent with _____ include money, shares, consumer goods through hire purchase, major assets such as aircraft, and even entire factories in finance lease arrangements.

    a. Interest
    b. A Random Walk Down Wall Street
    c. AAB
    d. Insolvency

13. An _____ is the price a borrower pays for the use of money they do not own, and the return a lender receives for deferring the use of funds, by lending it to the borrower. _____s are normally expressed as a percentage rate over the period of one year.

    _____s targets are also a vital tool of monetary policy and are used to control variables like investment, inflation, and unemployment.

    a. A Random Walk Down Wall Street
    b. ABN Amro
    c. AAB
    d. Interest rate

14. An _____ is a derivative in which one party exchanges a stream of interest payments for another party's stream of cash flows. _____s can be used by hedgers to manage their fixed or floating assets and liabilities. They can also be used by speculators to replicate unfunded bond exposures to profit from changes in interest rates.

    a. Equity swap
    b. International Swaps and Derivatives Association
    c. Implied volatility
    d. Interest rate swap

15. In finance, a _____ is a derivative in which two counterparties agree to exchange one stream of cash flows against another stream. These streams are called the legs of the _____.

Chapter 1. Introduction

The cash flows are calculated over a notional principal amount, which is usually not exchanged between counterparties.

a. Local volatility
b. Volatility arbitrage
c. Volatility swap
d. Swap

16. _____ is the discipline of identifying, monitoring and limiting risks. In some cases the acceptable risk may be near zero. Risks can come from accidents, natural causes and disasters as well as deliberate attacks from an adversary.

a. Risk management
b. 4-4-5 Calendar
c. FIFO
d. Penny stock

17. _____ (in a financial context) is the assumption of the risk of loss, in return for the uncertain possibility of a reward. Only if one may safely say that a particular position involves no risk may one say, strictly speaking, that such a position represents an 'investment.' Financial _____ involves the buying, holding, selling, and short-selling of stocks, bonds, commodities, currencies, collectibles, real estate, derivatives, or any valuable financial instrument to profit from fluctuations in its price as opposed to buying it for use or for income via methods such as dividends or interest. _____ represents one of four market roles in Western financial markets, distinct from hedging, long- or short-term investing, and arbitrage.

a. Forward market
b. Central Securities Depository
c. Market anomaly
d. Speculation

18. In economics and finance, _____ is the practice of taking advantage of a price differential between two or more markets: striking a combination of matching deals that capitalize upon the imbalance, the profit being the difference between the market prices. When used by academics, an _____ is a transaction that involves no negative cash flow at any probabilistic or temporal state and a positive cash flow in at least one state; in simple terms, a risk-free profit.

a. Initial margin
b. Efficient-market hypothesis
c. Arbitrage
d. Issuer

Chapter 2. Futures Markets

1. In finance, a _____ is a standardized contract, to buy or sell a specified commodity of standardized quality at a certain date in the future, at a market determined price (the futures price.)

    The price is determined by the instantaneous equilibrium between the forces of supply and demand among competing buy and sell orders on the exchange at the time of the purchase or sale of the contract.

    In many cases, the items may be such non-traditional 'commodities' as foreign currencies, commercial or government paper [e.g., bonds], or 'baskets' of corporate equity ['stock indices'] or other financial instruments.

    a. Repurchase agreement
    b. Heston model
    c. Financial future
    d. Futures contract

2. A _____ is an exchange of promises between two or more parties to do an act which is enforceable in a court of law. It is where an unqualified offer meets a qualified acceptance and the parties reach Consensus ad Idem. The parties must have the necessary capacity to _____ and the _____ must not be either trifling, indeterminate, impossible or illegal.

    a. Contract
    b. 7-Eleven
    c. 4-4-5 Calendar
    d. 529 plan

3. In banking and finance, _____ denotes all activities from the time a commitment is made for a transaction until it is settled. _____ is necessary because the speed of trades is much faster than the cycle time for completing the underlying transaction.

    In its widest sense _____ involves the management of post-trading, pre-settlement credit exposures, to ensure that trades are settled in accordance with market rules, even if a buyer or seller should become insolvent prior to settlement.

    a. Share
    b. Clearing
    c. Procter ' Gamble
    d. Clearing house

4. A _____ is a financial services company that provides clearing and settlement services for financial transactions, usually on a futures exchange, and often acts as central counterparty (the payor actually pays the _____, which then pays the payee). A _____ may also offer novation, the substitution of a new contract or debt for an old, or other credit enhancement services to its members.

Chapter 2. Futures Markets

The term is also used for banks like Suffolk Bank that acted as a restraint on the over-issuance of private bank notes.

a. Bucket shop
b. Clearing house
c. Warrant
d. Valuation

5. In finance, a _____ is collateral that the holder of a position in securities, options, or futures contracts has to deposit to cover the credit risk of his counterparty (most often his broker.) This risk can arise if the holder has done any of the following:

- borrowed cash from the counterparty to buy securities or options,
- sold securities or options short, or
- entered into a futures contract.

The collateral can be in the form of cash or securities, and it is deposited in a _____ account. On U.S. futures exchanges, '_____' was formally called performance bond.

_____ buying is buying securities with cash borrowed from a broker, using other securities as collateral.

a. Credit
b. Margin
c. Share
d. Procter ' Gamble

6. A _____ is a method of measuring a section of the stock market. Many indices are cited by news or financial services firms and are used to benchmark the performance of portfolios such as mutual funds.

a. Program trading
b. Stock market index
c. Stop order
d. Trading curb

7. In economics and finance, _____ is the practice of taking advantage of a price differential between two or more markets: striking a combination of matching deals that capitalize upon the imbalance, the profit being the difference between the market prices. When used by academics, an _____ is a transaction that involves no negative cash flow at any probabilistic or temporal state and a positive cash flow in at least one state; in simple terms, a risk-free profit.

Chapter 2. Futures Markets

a. Initial margin
b. Issuer
c. Efficient-market hypothesis
d. Arbitrage

8. In finance, a _____ is a position established in one market in an attempt to offset exposure to the price risk of an equal but opposite obligation or position in another market -- usually, but not always, in the context of one's commercial activity. Hedging is a strategy designed to minimize exposure to such business risks as a sharp contraction in demand for one's inventory, while still allowing the business to profit from producing and maintaining that inventory. A typical hedger might be a farmer with 2000 acres of unharvested wheat in the ground, who would rather tend his crop without the distraction of uncertain prices.

a. 4-4-5 Calendar
b. Hedge
c. 529 plan
d. 7-Eleven

9. The _____ is the amount required to be collateralized in order to open a position. Thereafter, the amount required to be kept in collateral until the position is closed is the maintenance requirement. The maintenance requirement is the minimum amount to be collateralized in order to keep an open position.

a. A Random Walk Down Wall Street
b. Initial margin requirement
c. ABN Amro
d. AAB

10. _____ is a method of hedging a portfolio of stocks against the market risk by short selling stock index futures. This hedging technique is frequently used by institutional investors when the market direction is uncertain or volatile. Short selling index futures can offset any downturns, but it also hinders any gains.

a. PAUG
b. Freight derivative
c. Delivery month
d. Portfolio insurance

11. The variation margin or _____ is not collateral, but a daily offsetting of profits and losses. Futures are marked-to-market every day, so the current price is compared to the previous day's price. The profit or loss on the day of a position is then paid to or debited from the holder by the futures exchange.

Chapter 2. Futures Markets

a. SPI 200 futures contract
b. Delivery month
c. Maintenance margin
d. Total return swap

12. _____ is the balance of the amounts of cash being received and paid by a business during a defined period of time, sometimes tied to a specific project. Measurement of _____ can be used

- to evaluate the state or performance of a business or project.
- to determine problems with liquidity. Being profitable does not necessarily mean being liquid. A company can fail because of a shortage of cash, even while profitable.
- to generate project rate of returns. The time of _____s into and out of projects are used as inputs to financial models such as internal rate of return, and net present value.
- to examine income or growth of a business when it is believed that accrual accounting concepts do not represent economic realities. Alternately, _____ can be used to 'validate' the net income generated by accrual accounting.

_____ as a generic term may be used differently depending on context, and certain _____ definitions may be adapted by analysts and users for their own uses. Common terms include operating _____ and free _____.

_____s can be classified into:

1. Operational _____s: Cash received or expended as a result of the company's core business activities.
2. Investment _____s: Cash received or expended through capital expenditure, investments or acquisitions.
3. Financing _____s: Cash received or expended as a result of financial activities, such as interests and dividends.

All three together - the net _____ - are necessary to reconcile the beginning cash balance to the ending cash balance. Loan draw downs or equity injections, that is just shifting of capital but no expenditure as such, are not considered in the net _____.

a. Corporate finance
b. Real option
c. Cash flow
d. Shareholder value

13. In business and accounting, _____s are everything of value that is owned by a person or company. The balance sheet of a firm records the monetary value of the _____s owned by the firm. The two major _____ classes are tangible _____s and intangible _____s.

Chapter 2. Futures Markets

a. Asset
b. Income
c. Accounts payable
d. EBITDA

14. A _____ is something for which there is demand, but which is supplied without qualitative differentiation across a market. It is a product that is the same no matter who produces it, such as petroleum, notebook paper, or milk. In other words, copper is copper.

   a. 4-4-5 Calendar
   b. 529 plan
   c. 7-Eleven
   d. Commodity

15. In business and finance, a _____ (also referred to as equity _____) of stock means a _____ of ownership in a corporation (company.) In the plural, stocks is often used as a synonym for _____s especially in the United States, but it is less commonly used that way outside of North America.

In the United Kingdom, South Africa, and Australia, stock can also refer to completely different financial instruments such as government bonds or, less commonly, to all kinds of marketable securities.

a. Margin
b. Procter ' Gamble
c. Bucket shop
d. Share

16. The _____ process is the process of determining the price of an asset in the marketplace through the interactions of buyers and sellers .

_____ is different from valuation. _____ process involves buyers and sellers arriving at a transaction price for a specific item at a given time.

   a. Price discovery
   b. Seed round
   c. Return on capital employed
   d. Pecking order theory

Chapter 2. Futures Markets

17. A _____ is a central financial exchange where people can trade standardized futures contracts; that is, a contract to buy specific quantities of a commodity or financial instrument at a specified price with delivery set at a specified time in the future.

Though the origins of futures trading can supposedly be traced to Ancient Greek or Phoenician times, the first modern organized _____ began in 1710 at the Dojima Rice Exchange in Osaka, Japan.

The United States followed in the early 1800s.

a. 4-4-5 Calendar
b. 7-Eleven
c. 529 plan
d. Futures exchange

18. A _____ is a member of an exchange who is an employee of a member firm and executes orders, as agent, on the floor of the exchange for clients. The _____ receives an order via teletype machine from his firm's trading department and then proceeds to the appropriate trading post on the exchange floor. There he joins other brokers and the specialist in the security being bought or sold and executes the trade at the best competitive price available.

a. Case-Shiller Home Price Indices
b. Floor broker
c. Multivariate normal distribution
d. Business valuation standards

19. 'A _____ is an individual or organization which operates or solicits funds for a commodity pool; that is, an enterprise in which funds contributed by a number of persons are combined for the purpose of trading futures contracts or commodity options, or to invest in another commodity pool.' National Futures Association (NFA) definition. The NFA regulates every firm or individual who conducts futures trading business with public customers.

A _____ will generally consist of an entity that accepts funds, securities or property for the purpose of trading commodity futures contracts.

a. Trading strategy
b. Regulation Fair Disclosure
c. Revenue recognition
d. Commodity Pool Operator

20. _____ has been viewed as a process of increasing involvement of enterprises in international markets, although there is no agreed definition of _____ or international entrepreneurship. There are several _____ theories which try to explain why there are international activities.

Chapter 2. Futures Markets

Adam Smith claimed that a country should specialise in, and export, commodities in which it had an absolute advantage.

a. AAB
b. A Random Walk Down Wall Street
c. ABN Amro
d. Internationalization

21. In economics, business, and accounting, a _____ is the value of money that has been used up to produce something, and hence is not available for use anymore. In business, the _____ may be one of acquisition, in which case the amount of money expended to acquire it is counted as _____. In this case, money is the input that is gone in order to acquire the thing.

a. Sliding scale fees
b. Marginal cost
c. Fixed costs
d. Cost

Chapter 3. Futures Prices

1. In finance, a _____ is a standardized contract, to buy or sell a specified commodity of standardized quality at a certain date in the future, at a market determined price (the futures price.)

   The price is determined by the instantaneous equilibrium between the forces of supply and demand among competing buy and sell orders on the exchange at the time of the purchase or sale of the contract.

   In many cases, the items may be such non-traditional 'commodities' as foreign currencies, commercial or government paper [e.g., bonds], or 'baskets' of corporate equity ['stock indices'] or other financial instruments.

   a. Heston model
   b. Financial future
   c. Repurchase agreement
   d. Futures contract

2. A _____ is an exchange of promises between two or more parties to do an act which is enforceable in a court of law. It is where an unqualified offer meets a qualified acceptance and the parties reach Consensus ad Idem. The parties must have the necessary capacity to _____ and the _____ must not be either trifling, indeterminate, impossible or illegal.

   a. 7-Eleven
   b. Contract
   c. 4-4-5 Calendar
   d. 529 plan

3. _____, in accrual accounting, is any account where the asset or liability is not realized until a future date, e.g. annuities, charges, taxes, income, etc. The _____ item may be carried, dependent on type of deferral, as either an asset or liability. See also: accrual

   _____ is also used in the university admissions process. It is the action by which a school rejects a student for early admission but still opts to review that student in the general admissions pool.

   a. Current asset
   b. Net profit
   c. Revenue
   d. Deferred

4. In the context of financial futures, _____ can be defined as the spot price minus the futures price. There will be a different basis for each delivery month for each contract. In a normal market, basis will be negative.

Chapter 3. Futures Prices

a. Legal and regulatory risk
b. Basis of futures
c. Controlled foreign corporations
d. Municipal Okrug #7

5. A _____ is heuristic and has the following assumptions :

- Rationality of all market actors (Rationality in meaning of the actor's utility maximization)
- No transaction costs (particularly no information costs and no taxes)
- Price taking behavior - there is a sufficiently large number of participants such that no individual can affect the market
- given rare resources
- freedom of decision to do something or to let it be (no external effects)

Share and foreign exchange markets are commonly seen to be the most similar to the _____. The real estate market is an example of a very imperfect market. a free market economy is also related to this _____ system as the public have free will

Other characteristics of a _____ include:-

- No barriers to entry to (or exit from) the market
- Perfect knowledge
- Normal profits

Normal profits are defined as that level of profit which just induces the participants to stay in the market. In other words companies in a _____ pay no dividends, as super-normal profits would induce other participants into the market and drive profits back to the 'normal' level.

This attribute of _____s has profound political and economic implications, as many people assume that the purpose of the market is to enable participants to make profits.

a. Perfect market
b. 4-4-5 Calendar
c. 7-Eleven
d. 529 plan

6. The official bank rate has existing in various forms since 1694 and has ranged from 0.5% to 17%. The name of this key interest rate has changed over the years. The current name 'Official Bank Rate' was introduced in 2006 and replaced the previous title '_____' (repo is short for repurchase agreement) in 1997.

Chapter 3. Futures Prices

   a. Repo rate
   b. London Interbank Offered Rate
   c. Cash accumulation equation
   d. London Interbank Bid Rate

7. A _____ allows a borrower to use a financial security as collateral for a cash loan at a fixed rate of interest. In a repo, the borrower agrees to immediately sell a security to a lender and also agrees to buy the same security from the lender at a fixed price at some later date. A repo is equivalent to a cash transaction combined with a forward contract.
   a. Volatility arbitrage
   b. Contango
   c. Repurchase agreement
   d. Total return swap

8. In economics and finance, _____ is the practice of taking advantage of a price differential between two or more markets: striking a combination of matching deals that capitalize upon the imbalance, the profit being the difference between the market prices. When used by academics, an _____ is a transaction that involves no negative cash flow at any probabilistic or temporal state and a positive cash flow in at least one state; in simple terms, a risk-free profit.
   a. Issuer
   b. Efficient-market hypothesis
   c. Initial margin
   d. Arbitrage

9. In economics, business, and accounting, a _____ is the value of money that has been used up to produce something, and hence is not available for use anymore. In business, the _____ may be one of acquisition, in which case the amount of money expended to acquire it is counted as _____. In this case, money is the input that is gone in order to acquire the thing.
   a. Sliding scale fees
   b. Cost
   c. Marginal cost
   d. Fixed costs

10. In economics and related disciplines, a _____ is a cost incurred in making an economic exchange. For example, most people, when buying or selling a stock, must pay a commission to their broker; that commission is a _____ of doing the stock deal. Or consider buying a banana from a store; to purchase the banana, your costs will be not only the price of the banana itself, but also the energy and effort it requires to find out which of the various banana products you prefer, where to get them and at what price, the cost of traveling from your house to the store and back, the time waiting in line, and the effort of the paying itself; the costs above and beyond the cost of the banana are the _____s.

Chapter 3. Futures Prices

a. Variable costs
b. Fixed costs
c. Transaction cost
d. Marginal cost

11. In financial mathematics, _____ are mathematical relationships specifying simple limits on derivative prices. Normally, these are found by simple arguments based on the payouts of the security in question, without specifying any sort of Distribution on any of the asset returns involved.

Lack of arbitrage explains some rather obvious questions in option pricing, such that the value of a call option will never rise above the underlying stock price itself.

a. No-arbitrage bounds
b. Death spiral financing
c. Primary market
d. Convenience translation

12. In finance, _____ or 'shorting' is the practice of selling a financial instrument that the seller does not own at the time of the sale. _____ is done with intent of later purchasing the financial instrument at a lower price. Short-sellers attempt to profit from an expected decline in the price of a financial instrument.

a. 529 plan
b. 4-4-5 Calendar
c. Short ratio
d. Short selling

13. The _____ of an asset is the return obtained from holding it (if positive), or the cost of holding it (if negative)

For instance, commodities are usually negative _____ assets, as they incur storage costs, but in some circumstances, commodities can be positive _____ assets as the market is willing to pay a premium for availability.

This can also refer to a trade with more than one leg, where you earn the spread between borrowing a low _____ asset and lending a high _____ one.

a. Carry
b. Bankruptcy remote
c. Financial assistance
d. Cramdown

Chapter 3. Futures Prices

14. A _____ is an adjustment to the cost of carry in the non-arbitrage pricing formula for forward prices in markets with trading constraints.

Let $F_{t,T}$ be the forward price of an asset with initial price S_t and maturity T. Suppose that r is the continuously compounded interest rate for one year. Then, the non-arbitrage pricing formula should be

$F_{t,T} = S_t e^{r(T >- t)}$.

a. 529 plan
b. 7-Eleven
c. 4-4-5 Calendar
d. Convenience yield

15. In finance, the term _____ describes the amount in cash that returns to the owners of a security. Normally it does not include the price variations, at the difference of the total return. _____ applies to various stated rates of return on stocks (common and preferred, and convertible), fixed income instruments (bonds, notes, bills, strips, zero coupon), and some other investment type insurance products (e.g. annuities.)

a. Yield
b. Yield to maturity
c. Macaulay duration
d. 4-4-5 Calendar

16. _____ (in a financial context) is the assumption of the risk of loss, in return for the uncertain possibility of a reward. Only if one may safely say that a particular position involves no risk may one say, strictly speaking, that such a position represents an 'investment.' Financial _____ involves the buying, holding, selling, and short-selling of stocks, bonds, commodities, currencies, collectibles, real estate, derivatives, or any valuable financial instrument to profit from fluctuations in its price as opposed to buying it for use or for income via methods such as dividends or interest. _____ represents one of four market roles in Western financial markets, distinct from hedging, long- or short-term investing, and arbitrage.

a. Forward market
b. Market anomaly
c. Speculation
d. Central Securities Depository

17. _____ is a concept in economics, finance, and psychology related to the behaviour of consumers and investors under uncertainty. _____ is the reluctance of a person to accept a bargain with an uncertain payoff rather than another bargain with a more certain, but possibly lower, expected payoff.

The inverse of a person's _____ is sometimes called their risk tolerance

Chapter 3. Futures Prices

a. Risk aversion
b. Discount factor
c. Risk adjusted return on capital
d. Risk premium

18. In business and accounting, _____s are everything of value that is owned by a person or company. The balance sheet of a firm records the monetary value of the _____s owned by the firm. The two major _____ classes are tangible _____s and intangible _____s.
    a. Accounts payable
    b. Asset
    c. Income
    d. EBITDA

19. In finance, _____ is the process of estimating the potential market value of a financial asset or liability. they can be done on assets (for example, investments in marketable securities such as stocks, options, business enterprises, or intangible assets such as patents and trademarks) or on liabilities (e.g., Bonds issued by a company.) _____s are required in many contexts including investment analysis, capital budgeting, merger and acquisition transactions, financial reporting, taxable events to determine the proper tax liability, and in litigation.
    a. Share
    b. Margin
    c. Procter ' Gamble
    d. Valuation

Chapter 3. Futures Prices

20. The term _____ has three unrelated technical definitions, and is also used in a variety of non-technical ways.

- In financial economics, it refers to any asset used to make money, as opposed to assets used for personal enjoyment or consumption. This is an important distinction because two people can disagree sharply about the value of personal assets, one person might think a sports car is more valuable than a pickup truck, another person might have the opposite taste. But if an asset is held for the purpose of making money, taste has nothing to do with it, only differences of opinion about how much money the asset will produce. With the further assumption that people agree on the probability distribution of future cash flows, it is possible to have an objective _____ pricing model. Even without the assumption of agreement, it is possible to set rational limits on _____ value.
- In governmental accounting, it is defined as any asset used in operations with an initial useful life extending beyond one reporting period. Generally, government managers have a 'stewardship' duty to maintain _____s under their control. See International Public Sector Accounting Standards for details.
- In US tax accounting, it is defined as any property other than a list of exceptions. The main exceptions are anything held for sale, and any real estate or depreciable property used in business. Almost everything you own and use for personal purposes, pleasure or investment is a _____. If something is a _____ for tax purposes, gains or losses on sale or disposition are capital gains or capital losses. For individuals, however, capital losses on property held for personal use are generally not deductible. See the IRS publication Tax Facts about Capital Gains and Losses for details.

A well-known financial accounting textbook advises that the term be avoided except in tax accounting because it is used in so many different senses, not all of them well-defined. For example it is often used as a synonym for fixed assets or for investments in securities.

A common non-technical usage occurs when people ask that employees or the environment or something else be treated as a _____.

a. Capital asset
b. Political risk
c. Solvency
d. Settlement date

21. The _____ or forward rate is the agreed upon price of an asset in a forward contract. Using the rational pricing assumption, we can express the _____ in terms of the spot price and any dividends etc., so that there is no possibility for arbitrage.

The _____ is given by:

Chapter 3. Futures Prices

where

F is the _____ to be paid at time T
e^x is the exponential function
r is the risk-free interest rate
q is the cost-of-carry
S_0 is the spot price of the asset (i.e. what it would sell for at time 0)
D_i is a dividend which is guaranteed to be paid at time t_i where $0 < t_i < T$.

The two questions here are what price the short position (the seller of the asset) should offer to maximize his gain, and what price the long position (the buyer of the asset) should accept to maximize his gain?

At the very least we know that both do not want to lose any money in the deal.

a. Biweekly Mortgage
b. Forward price
c. Security interest
d. Financial Gerontology

22. _____ is a mathematical tool for finding repeating patterns, such as the presence of a periodic signal which has been buried under noise, or identifying the missing fundamental frequency in a signal implied by its harmonic frequencies. It is used frequently in signal processing for analyzing functions or series of values, such as time domain signals. Informally, it is the similarity between observations as a function of the time separation between them.

a. AAB
b. A Random Walk Down Wall Street
c. ABN Amro
d. Autocorrelation

23. _____ most frequently refers to the standard deviation of the continuously compounded returns of a financial instrument with a specific time horizon. It is often used to quantify the risk of the instrument over that time period. _____ is typically expressed in annualized terms, and it may either be an absolute number ($5) or a fraction of the mean (5%).

a. Portfolio insurance
b. Currency swap
c. Volatility
d. Seasoned equity offering

Chapter 4. Using Futures Markets

1. In finance, a _____ is a standardized contract, to buy or sell a specified commodity of standardized quality at a certain date in the future, at a market determined price (the futures price.)

   The price is determined by the instantaneous equilibrium between the forces of supply and demand among competing buy and sell orders on the exchange at the time of the purchase or sale of the contract.

   In many cases, the items may be such non-traditional 'commodities' as foreign currencies, commercial or government paper [e.g., bonds], or 'baskets' of corporate equity ['stock indices'] or other financial instruments.

   a. Repurchase agreement
   b. Financial future
   c. Heston model
   d. Futures contract

2. The _____ process is the process of determining the price of an asset in the marketplace through the interactions of buyers and sellers.

   _____ is different from valuation. _____ process involves buyers and sellers arriving at a transaction price for a specific item at a given time.

   a. Seed round
   b. Pecking order theory
   c. Return on capital employed
   d. Price discovery

3. _____ (in a financial context) is the assumption of the risk of loss, in return for the uncertain possibility of a reward. Only if one may safely say that a particular position involves no risk may one say, strictly speaking, that such a position represents an 'investment.' Financial _____ involves the buying, holding, selling, and short-selling of stocks, bonds, commodities, currencies, collectibles, real estate, derivatives, or any valuable financial instrument to profit from fluctuations in its price as opposed to buying it for use or for income via methods such as dividends or interest. _____ represents one of four market roles in Western financial markets, distinct from hedging, long- or short-term investing, and arbitrage.

   a. Market anomaly
   b. Forward market
   c. Central Securities Depository
   d. Speculation

4. A _____ is a trader who buys and sells financial instruments (eg stocks, options, futures, derivatives, currencies) within the same trading day such that all positions will usually be closed before the market close of the trading day. This trading style is called day trading. Depending on one's trading strategy, it may range from several to hundreds of orders a day.

Chapter 4. Using Futures Markets

a. Stockbroker
b. Financial analyst
c. Portfolio manager
d. Day trader

5. In options trading, a _____ (sometimes simply butterfly) is a combination trade resulting in the following net position:

   - Long 1 call at (X − a) strike
   - Short 2 calls at X strike
   - Long 1 call at (X + a) strike

   all with the same expiration date. At expiration the position will be worth zero if the underlying is below X−a or above X+a, and will be worth a positive amount between these two values. The payoff function is shaped like an upside-down V, and the maximum payoff occurs at X

   Since the payoff is sometimes zero, sometimes positive, the price of a butterfly is always non-negative (to avoid an arbitrage opportunity.)

   a. Long butterfly
   b. Naked put
   c. Bear spread
   d. Binary option

6. _____ is the difference between price and the costs of bringing to market whatever it is that is accounted as an enterprise (whether by harvest, extraction, manufacture, or purchase) in terms of the component costs of delivered goods and/or services and any operating or other expenses.

   A key difficulty in measuring profit is in defining costs. Pure economic monetary profits can be zero or negative even in competitive equilibrium when accounted monetized costs exceed monetized price.

   a. A Random Walk Down Wall Street
   b. Economic profit
   c. AAB
   d. Accounting profit

7. A _____ is something for which there is demand, but which is supplied without qualitative differentiation across a market. It is a product that is the same no matter who produces it, such as petroleum, notebook paper, or milk. In other words, copper is copper.

Chapter 4. Using Futures Markets

a. 529 plan
b. 4-4-5 Calendar
c. 7-Eleven
d. Commodity

8. In finance, a _____ is a position established in one market in an attempt to offset exposure to the price risk of an equal but opposite obligation or position in another market -- usually, but not always, in the context of one's commercial activity. Hedging is a strategy designed to minimize exposure to such business risks as a sharp contraction in demand for one's inventory, while still allowing the business to profit from producing and maintaining that inventory. A typical hedger might be a farmer with 2000 acres of unharvested wheat in the ground, who would rather tend his crop without the distraction of uncertain prices.

a. Hedge
b. 529 plan
c. 7-Eleven
d. 4-4-5 Calendar

9. In economics, business, and accounting, a _____ is the value of money that has been used up to produce something, and hence is not available for use anymore. In business, the _____ may be one of acquisition, in which case the amount of money expended to acquire it is counted as _____. In this case, money is the input that is gone in order to acquire the thing.

a. Cost
b. Sliding scale fees
c. Fixed costs
d. Marginal cost

10. _____ is a term in Corporate Finance used to indicate a condition when promises to creditors of a company are broken or honored with difficulty. Sometimes _____ can lead to bankruptcy. _____ is usually associated with some costs to the company and these are known as Costs of _____.

a. Capital structure
b. Commercial paper
c. Cashflow matching
d. Financial distress

Chapter 4. Using Futures Markets

11. In economics and related disciplines, a _____ is a cost incurred in making an economic exchange. For example, most people, when buying or selling a stock, must pay a commission to their broker; that commission is a _____ of doing the stock deal. Or consider buying a banana from a store; to purchase the banana, your costs will be not only the price of the banana itself, but also the energy and effort it requires to find out which of the various banana products you prefer, where to get them and at what price, the cost of traveling from your house to the store and back, the time waiting in line, and the effort of the paying itself; the costs above and beyond the cost of the banana are the _____s.

   a. Fixed costs
   b. Variable costs
   c. Marginal cost
   d. Transaction cost

12. _____ in finance is a risk management technique, related to hedging, that mixes a wide variety of investments within a portfolio. Because the fluctuations of a single security have less impact on a diverse portfolio, _____ minimizes the risk from any one investment.

   A simple example of _____ is the following: On a particular island the entire economy consists of two companies: one that sells umbrellas and another that sells sunscreen.

   a. 7-Eleven
   b. Diversification
   c. 4-4-5 Calendar
   d. 529 plan

Chapter 5. Interest Rate Futures: Introduction

1. _____ is a fee paid on borrowed assets. It is the price paid for the use of borrowed money, or, money earned by deposited funds. Assets that are sometimes lent with _____ include money, shares, consumer goods through hire purchase, major assets such as aircraft, and even entire factories in finance lease arrangements.
   a. AAB
   b. Interest
   c. Insolvency
   d. A Random Walk Down Wall Street

2. An _____ is the price a borrower pays for the use of money they do not own, and the return a lender receives for deferring the use of funds, by lending it to the borrower. _____s are normally expressed as a percentage rate over the period of one year.

   _____s targets are also a vital tool of monetary policy and are used to control variables like investment, inflation, and unemployment.

   a. ABN Amro
   b. AAB
   c. Interest rate
   d. A Random Walk Down Wall Street

3. An _____ is a futures contract with an interest-bearing instrument as the underlying asset.

   Examples include Treasury-bill futures, Treasury-bond futures and Eurodollar futures.

   The global market for exchange-traded _____s is notionally valued by the Bank for International Settlements at $5,794,200 million in 2005.

   a. Interest rate derivative
   b. Open interest
   c. Interest rate future
   d. Equity swap

4. _____ mature in one year or less. Like zero-coupon bonds, they do not pay interest prior to maturity; instead they are sold at a discount of the par value to create a positive yield to maturity. Many regard _____ as the least risky investment available to U.S. investors.
   a. Treasury securities
   b. 4-4-5 Calendar
   c. Treasury Inflation Protected Securities
   d. Treasury bills

Chapter 5. Interest Rate Futures: Introduction

5. A _____ is an exchange of promises between two or more parties to do an act which is enforceable in a court of law. It is where an unqualified offer meets a qualified acceptance and the parties reach Consensus ad Idem. The parties must have the necessary capacity to _____ and the _____ must not be either trifling, indeterminate, impossible or illegal.

   a. 7-Eleven
   b. 529 plan
   c. 4-4-5 Calendar
   d. Contract

6. In finance, a _____ is a standardized contract, to buy or sell a specified commodity of standardized quality at a certain date in the future, at a market determined price (the futures price.)

   The price is determined by the instantaneous equilibrium between the forces of supply and demand among competing buy and sell orders on the exchange at the time of the purchase or sale of the contract.

   In many cases, the items may be such non-traditional 'commodities' as foreign currencies, commercial or government paper [e.g., bonds], or 'baskets' of corporate equity ['stock indices'] or other financial instruments.

   a. Repurchase agreement
   b. Heston model
   c. Financial future
   d. Futures contract

7. _____s are deposits denominated in United States dollars at banks outside the United States, and thus are not under the jurisdiction of the Federal Reserve. Consequently, such deposits are subject to much less regulation than similar deposits within the United States, allowing for higher margins. There is nothing 'European' about _____ deposits; a US dollar-denominated deposit in Tokyo or Caracas would likewise be deemed _____ deposits.

   a. A Random Walk Down Wall Street
   b. ABN Amro
   c. AAB
   d. Eurodollar

8. In finance, the _____ is the global financial market for short-term borrowing and lending. It provides short-term liquidity funding for the global financial system. The _____ is where short-term obligations such as Treasury bills, commercial paper and bankers' acceptances are bought and sold.

Chapter 5. Interest Rate Futures: Introduction

27

a. Debt-for-equity swap
b. Money market
c. Consumer debt
d. Cramdown

9. In finance, a _____ is a debt security, in which the authorized issuer owes the holders a debt and, depending on the terms of the _____, is obliged to pay interest (the coupon) and/or to repay the principal at a later date, termed maturity. Thus a _____ is a loan: the issuer is the borrower, the _____ holder is the lender, and the coupon is the interest. _____s provide the borrower with external funds to finance long-term investments, or, in the case of government _____s, to finance current expenditure.

a. Bond
b. Convertible bond
c. Puttable bond
d. Catastrophe bonds

10. _____ are government bonds issued by the United States Department of the Treasury through the Bureau of the Public Debt. They are the debt financing instruments of the U.S. Federal government, and they are often referred to simply as Treasuries or Treasurys. There are four types of marketable _____: Treasury bills, Treasury notes, Treasury bonds, and Treasury Inflation Protected Securities (TIPS.)

a. Treasury Inflation Protected Securities
b. Treasury securities
c. 4-4-5 Calendar
d. Treasury Inflation-Protected Securities

11. A _____ is a financial contract whose value is derived from the value of something else (known as the underlying.) The underlying on which a _____ is based can be an asset, weather conditions bonds or other forms of credit.

a. Derivative
b. 7-Eleven
c. 4-4-5 Calendar
d. 529 plan

12. _____ is a life of security. It may also refer to the final payment date of a loan or other financial instrument, at which point all remaining interest and principal is due to be paid.

Chapter 5. Interest Rate Futures: Introduction

1, 3, 6 months _____ band can be calculated by using 30-day per month periods.

    a. False billing
    b. Replacement cost
    c. Maturity
    d. Primary market

13. A _____ is heuristic and has the following assumptions :

- Rationality of all market actors (Rationality in meaning of the actor's utility maximization)
- No transaction costs (particularly no information costs and no taxes)
- Price taking behavior - there is a sufficiently large number of participants such that no individual can affect the market
- given rare resources
- freedom of decision to do something or to let it be (no external effects)

Share and foreign exchange markets are commonly seen to be the most similar to the _____. The real estate market is an example of a very imperfect market. a free market economy is also related to this _____ system as the public have free will

Other characteristics of a _____ include:-

- No barriers to entry to (or exit from) the market
- Perfect knowledge
- Normal profits

Normal profits are defined as that level of profit which just induces the participants to stay in the market. In other words companies in a _____ pay no dividends, as super-normal profits would induce other participants into the market and drive profits back to the 'normal' level.

This attribute of _____s has profound political and economic implications, as many people assume that the purpose of the market is to enable participants to make profits.

    a. 7-Eleven
    b. Perfect market
    c. 529 plan
    d. 4-4-5 Calendar

14. The _____ or forward rate is the agreed upon price of an asset in a forward contract. Using the rational pricing assumption, we can express the _____ in terms of the spot price and any dividends etc., so that there is no possibility for arbitrage.

Chapter 5. Interest Rate Futures: Introduction

The _____ is given by:

$$F > \text{...}$$

where

    F is the _____ to be paid at time T
    e^x is the exponential function
    r is the risk-free interest rate
    q is the cost-of-carry
    S_0 is the spot price of the asset (i.e. what it would sell for at time 0)
    D_i is a dividend which is guaranteed to be paid at time t_i where $0 < t_i < T$.

The two questions here are what price the short position (the seller of the asset) should offer to maximize his gain, and what price the long position (the buyer of the asset) should accept to maximize his gain?

At the very least we know that both do not want to lose any money in the deal.

    a. Financial Gerontology
    b. Security interest
    c. Biweekly Mortgage
    d. Forward price

15. In finance, the term _____ describes the amount in cash that returns to the owners of a security. Normally it does not include the price variations, at the difference of the total return. _____ applies to various stated rates of return on stocks (common and preferred, and convertible), fixed income instruments (bonds, notes, bills, strips, zero coupon), and some other investment type insurance products (e.g. annuities.)

    a. 4-4-5 Calendar
    b. Yield
    c. Macaulay duration
    d. Yield to maturity

16. In finance, a _____ is a position established in one market in an attempt to offset exposure to the price risk of an equal but opposite obligation or position in another market -- usually, but not always, in the context of one's commercial activity. Hedging is a strategy designed to minimize exposure to such business risks as a sharp contraction in demand for one's inventory, while still allowing the business to profit from producing and maintaining that inventory. A typical hedger might be a farmer with 2000 acres of unharvested wheat in the ground, who would rather tend his crop without the distraction of uncertain prices.

a. 7-Eleven
b. 4-4-5 Calendar
c. 529 plan
d. Hedge

Chapter 6. Interest Rate Futures: Refinements

1. _____ is a fee paid on borrowed assets. It is the price paid for the use of borrowed money, or, money earned by deposited funds. Assets that are sometimes lent with _____ include money, shares, consumer goods through hire purchase, major assets such as aircraft, and even entire factories in finance lease arrangements.
   a. AAB
   b. A Random Walk Down Wall Street
   c. Insolvency
   d. Interest

2. An _____ is the price a borrower pays for the use of money they do not own, and the return a lender receives for deferring the use of funds, by lending it to the borrower. _____s are normally expressed as a percentage rate over the period of one year.

   _____s targets are also a vital tool of monetary policy and are used to control variables like investment, inflation, and unemployment.

   a. A Random Walk Down Wall Street
   b. AAB
   c. Interest rate
   d. ABN Amro

3. An _____ is a futures contract with an interest-bearing instrument as the underlying asset.

   Examples include Treasury-bill futures, Treasury-bond futures and Eurodollar futures.

   The global market for exchange-traded _____s is notionally valued by the Bank for International Settlements at $5,794,200 million in 2005.

   a. Interest rate future
   b. Interest rate derivative
   c. Open interest
   d. Equity swap

4. In finance, a _____ is a standardized contract, to buy or sell a specified commodity of standardized quality at a certain date in the future, at a market determined price (the futures price.)

   The price is determined by the instantaneous equilibrium between the forces of supply and demand among competing buy and sell orders on the exchange at the time of the purchase or sale of the contract.

   In many cases, the items may be such non-traditional 'commodities' as foreign currencies, commercial or government paper [e.g., bonds], or 'baskets' of corporate equity ['stock indices'] or other financial instruments.

Chapter 6. Interest Rate Futures: Refinements

   a. Financial future
   b. Heston model
   c. Repurchase agreement
   d. Futures contract

5. A _____ is an exchange of promises between two or more parties to do an act which is enforceable in a court of law. It is where an unqualified offer meets a qualified acceptance and the parties reach Consensus ad Idem. The parties must have the necessary capacity to _____ and the _____ must not be either trifling, indeterminate, impossible or illegal.

   a. 4-4-5 Calendar
   b. 529 plan
   c. 7-Eleven
   d. Contract

6. The coupon or _____ of a bond is the amount of interest paid per year expressed as a percentage of the face value of the bond.

   For example if you hold $10,000 nominal of a bond described as a 4.5% loan stock, you will receive $450 in interest each year (probably in two installments of $225 each.)

   Not all bonds have coupons.

   a. Coupon rate
   b. Puttable bond
   c. Zero-coupon bond
   d. Revenue bonds

7. In economics and finance, _____ is the practice of taking advantage of a price differential between two or more markets: striking a combination of matching deals that capitalize upon the imbalance, the profit being the difference between the market prices. When used by academics, an _____ is a transaction that involves no negative cash flow at any probabilistic or temporal state and a positive cash flow in at least one state; in simple terms, a risk-free profit.

   a. Arbitrage
   b. Issuer
   c. Efficient-market hypothesis
   d. Initial margin

8. In finance, _____ is the risk involved in using models to value financial securities. Rebonato considers alternative definitions including:

Chapter 6. Interest Rate Futures: Refinements

1) After observing a set of prices for the underlying and hedging instruments, different but identically calibrated models might produce different prices for the same exotic product. 2) Losses will be incurred because of an 'incorrect' hedging strategy suggested by a model.

   a. Duty of loyalty
   b. Takeover
   c. Price-to-book ratio
   d. Model risk

9. An _____ is a contract written by a seller that conveys to the buyer the right -- but not the obligation -- to buy (in the case of a call _____) or to sell (in the case of a put _____) a particular asset, such as a piece of property such as, among others, a futures contract. In return for granting the _____, the seller collects a payment (the premium) from the buyer.

   For example, buying a call _____ provides the right to buy a specified quantity of a security at a set strike price at some time on or before expiration, while buying a put _____ provides the right to sell.

   a. AT'T Mobility LLC
   b. Annuity
   c. Amortization
   d. Option

10. In economics, business, and accounting, a _____ is the value of money that has been used up to produce something, and hence is not available for use anymore. In business, the _____ may be one of acquisition, in which case the amount of money expended to acquire it is counted as _____. In this case, money is the input that is gone in order to acquire the thing.

    a. Fixed costs
    b. Sliding scale fees
    c. Cost
    d. Marginal cost

11. In economics and related disciplines, a _____ is a cost incurred in making an economic exchange. For example, most people, when buying or selling a stock, must pay a commission to their broker; that commission is a _____ of doing the stock deal. Or consider buying a banana from a store; to purchase the banana, your costs will be not only the price of the banana itself, but also the energy and effort it requires to find out which of the various banana products you prefer, where to get them and at what price, the cost of traveling from your house to the store and back, the time waiting in line, and the effort of the paying itself; the costs above and beyond the cost of the banana are the _____s.

Chapter 6. Interest Rate Futures: Refinements

a. Variable costs
b. Marginal cost
c. Fixed costs
d. Transaction cost

12. _____s are deposits denominated in United States dollars at banks outside the United States, and thus are not under the jurisdiction of the Federal Reserve. Consequently, such deposits are subject to much less regulation than similar deposits within the United States, allowing for higher margins. There is nothing 'European' about _____ deposits; a US dollar-denominated deposit in Tokyo or Caracas would likewise be deemed _____ deposits.

a. A Random Walk Down Wall Street
b. AAB
c. ABN Amro
d. Eurodollar

13. _____ mature in one year or less. Like zero-coupon bonds, they do not pay interest prior to maturity; instead they are sold at a discount of the par value to create a positive yield to maturity. Many regard _____ as the least risky investment available to U.S. investors.

a. 4-4-5 Calendar
b. Treasury securities
c. Treasury Inflation Protected Securities
d. Treasury bills

14. _____ is a life of security. It may also refer to the final payment date of a loan or other financial instrument, at which point all remaining interest and principal is due to be paid.

1, 3, 6 months _____ band can be calculated by using 30-day per month periods.

a. Primary market
b. Maturity
c. False billing
d. Replacement cost

15. In finance, a _____ is a position established in one market in an attempt to offset exposure to the price risk of an equal but opposite obligation or position in another market -- usually, but not always, in the context of one's commercial activity. Hedging is a strategy designed to minimize exposure to such business risks as a sharp contraction in demand for one's inventory, while still allowing the business to profit from producing and maintaining that inventory. A typical hedger might be a farmer with 2000 acres of unharvested wheat in the ground, who would rather tend his crop without the distraction of uncertain prices.

Chapter 6. Interest Rate Futures: Refinements

a. 529 plan
b. 4-4-5 Calendar
c. 7-Eleven
d. Hedge

Chapter 7. Stock Index Futures: Introduction

1. A _____ is a method of measuring a section of the stock market. Many indices are cited by news or financial services firms and are used to benchmark the performance of portfolios such as mutual funds.
   a. Trading curb
   b. Stock market index
   c. Stop order
   d. Program trading

2. In finance, a _____ is a standardized contract, to buy or sell a specified commodity of standardized quality at a certain date in the future, at a market determined price (the futures price.)

   The price is determined by the instantaneous equilibrium between the forces of supply and demand among competing buy and sell orders on the exchange at the time of the purchase or sale of the contract.

   In many cases, the items may be such non-traditional 'commodities' as foreign currencies, commercial or government paper [e.g., bonds], or 'baskets' of corporate equity ['stock indices'] or other financial instruments.

   a. Repurchase agreement
   b. Financial future
   c. Futures contract
   d. Heston model

3. In finance, a _____ is a position established in one market in an attempt to offset exposure to the price risk of an equal but opposite obligation or position in another market -- usually, but not always, in the context of one's commercial activity. Hedging is a strategy designed to minimize exposure to such business risks as a sharp contraction in demand for one's inventory, while still allowing the business to profit from producing and maintaining that inventory. A typical hedger might be a farmer with 2000 acres of unharvested wheat in the ground, who would rather tend his crop without the distraction of uncertain prices.
   a. 529 plan
   b. 4-4-5 Calendar
   c. Hedge
   d. 7-Eleven

4. A _____ index is a stock market index where each constituent makes up a fraction of the index that is proportional to its price. For a stock market index this implies that stocks are included in proportions based on their quoted prices. A stock trading at $100 will thus be making up 10 times more of the total index compared to a stock trading at $10.
   a. Trade finance
   b. Product life cycle
   c. Golden parachute
   d. Price-weighted

Chapter 7. Stock Index Futures: Introduction

5. The _____ on a portfolio of investments takes into account not only the capital appreciation on the portfolio, but also the income received on the portfolio. The income typically consists of interest, dividends, and securities lending fees. This contrasts with the price return, which takes into account only the capital gain on an investment.
   a. Capitalization rate
   b. Global tactical asset allocation
   c. Total return
   d. Profitability index

6. A _____ is an exchange of promises between two or more parties to do an act which is enforceable in a court of law. It is where an unqualified offer meets a qualified acceptance and the parties reach Consensus ad Idem. The parties must have the necessary capacity to _____ and the _____ must not be either trifling, indeterminate, impossible or illegal.
   a. 4-4-5 Calendar
   b. Contract
   c. 529 plan
   d. 7-Eleven

7. _____, also called fair price (in a commonplace conflation of the two distinct concepts), is a concept used in finance and economics, defined as a rational and unbiased estimate of the potential market price of a good, service, or asset, taking into account such objective factors as:

   - acquisition/production/distribution costs, replacement costs, or costs of close substitutes
   - actual utility at a given level of development of social productive capability
   - supply vs. demand

   and subjective factors such as

   - risk characteristics
   - cost of capital
   - individually perceived utility

In accounting, _____ is used as an estimate of the market value of an asset (or liability) for which a market price cannot be determined (usually because there is no established market for the asset.) Under GAAP (FAS 157), _____ is the amount at which the asset could be bought or sold in a current transaction between willing parties, or transferred to an equivalent party, other than in a liquidation sale. This is used for assets whose carrying value is based on mark-to-market valuations; for assets carried at historical cost, the _____ of the asset is not used. One example of where _____ is an issue is a College kitchen with a cost of $2 million which was built 5 years ago.

Chapter 7. Stock Index Futures: Introduction

a. 7-Eleven
b. 529 plan
c. 4-4-5 Calendar
d. Fair value

8. In economics and finance, _____ is the practice of taking advantage of a price differential between two or more markets: striking a combination of matching deals that capitalize upon the imbalance, the profit being the difference between the market prices. When used by academics, an _____ is a transaction that involves no negative cash flow at any probabilistic or temporal state and a positive cash flow in at least one state; in simple terms, a risk-free profit.

a. Arbitrage
b. Issuer
c. Initial margin
d. Efficient-market hypothesis

9. _____ is casually defined as the use of computers in stock markets to engage in arbitrage and portfolio insurance strategies. However, the New York Stock Exchange (NYSE) defines the term as 'a wide range of portfolio trading strategies involving the purchase or sale of 15 or more stocks having a total market value of $1 million or more' without any direct reference to the use of computers. The word 'program' can be interpreted in its earlier, more general meaning of a defined and pre-arranged sequence of steps, rather than specifically a computer program.

a. Stop order
b. Share price
c. Wash sale
d. Program trading

10. A _____ is a payment made by a corporation to its shareholder members. When a corporation earns a profit or surplus, that money can be put to two uses: it can either be re-invested in the business (called retained earnings), or it can be paid to the shareholders as a _____. Many corporations retain a portion of their earnings and pay the remainder as a _____.

a. Dividend yield
b. Special dividend
c. Dividend
d. Dividend puzzle

11. _____ is a political organization established in 2002 and dedicated to the protection of children from abuse, exploitation and neglect. It is a nonprofit, 501(c)(4) membership association with members in every U.S. state and 10 nations. _____ achieved great success in its first three years, winning legislative victories in eight state legislatures.

Chapter 7. Stock Index Futures: Introduction

a. First Prudential Markets
b. The Depository Trust ' Clearing Corporation
c. Ford Foundation
d. Protect

12. _____ is the discipline of identifying, monitoring and limiting risks. In some cases the acceptable risk may be near zero. Risks can come from accidents, natural causes and disasters as well as deliberate attacks from an adversary.
a. Risk management
b. 4-4-5 Calendar
c. Penny stock
d. FIFO

Chapter 8. Stock Index Futures: Refinements

1. A _____ is a method of measuring a section of the stock market. Many indices are cited by news or financial services firms and are used to benchmark the performance of portfolios such as mutual funds.
   a. Program trading
   b. Trading curb
   c. Stop order
   d. Stock market index

2. In finance, a _____ is a standardized contract, to buy or sell a specified commodity of standardized quality at a certain date in the future, at a market determined price (the futures price.)

   The price is determined by the instantaneous equilibrium between the forces of supply and demand among competing buy and sell orders on the exchange at the time of the purchase or sale of the contract.

   In many cases, the items may be such non-traditional 'commodities' as foreign currencies, commercial or government paper [e.g., bonds], or 'baskets' of corporate equity ['stock indices'] or other financial instruments.

   a. Repurchase agreement
   b. Financial future
   c. Heston model
   d. Futures contract

3. In finance, a _____ is a position established in one market in an attempt to offset exposure to the price risk of an equal but opposite obligation or position in another market -- usually, but not always, in the context of one's commercial activity. Hedging is a strategy designed to minimize exposure to such business risks as a sharp contraction in demand for one's inventory, while still allowing the business to profit from producing and maintaining that inventory. A typical hedger might be a farmer with 2000 acres of unharvested wheat in the ground, who would rather tend his crop without the distraction of uncertain prices.
   a. 4-4-5 Calendar
   b. 529 plan
   c. 7-Eleven
   d. Hedge

4. _____ is casually defined as the use of computers in stock markets to engage in arbitrage and portfolio insurance strategies. However, the New York Stock Exchange (NYSE) defines the term as 'a wide range of portfolio trading strategies involving the purchase or sale of 15 or more stocks having a total market value of $1 million or more' without any direct reference to the use of computers. The word 'program' can be interpreted in its earlier, more general meaning of a defined and pre-arranged sequence of steps, rather than specifically a computer program.

Chapter 8. Stock Index Futures: Refinements

a. Wash sale
b. Stop order
c. Share price
d. Program trading

5. In economics and finance, _____ is the practice of taking advantage of a price differential between two or more markets: striking a combination of matching deals that capitalize upon the imbalance, the profit being the difference between the market prices. When used by academics, an _____ is a transaction that involves no negative cash flow at any probabilistic or temporal state and a positive cash flow in at least one state; in simple terms, a risk-free profit.

a. Issuer
b. Initial margin
c. Efficient-market hypothesis
d. Arbitrage

6. In business and accounting, _____s are everything of value that is owned by a person or company. The balance sheet of a firm records the monetary value of the _____s owned by the firm. The two major _____ classes are tangible _____s and intangible _____s.

a. Asset
b. EBITDA
c. Income
d. Accounts payable

7. _____ is a term used to refer to how an investor distributes his or her investments among various classes of investment vehicles (e.g., stocks and bonds.)

A large part of financial planning is finding an _____ that is appropriate for a given person in terms of their appetite for and ability to shoulder risk. This can depend on various factors; see investor profile.

a. Investing online
b. Alternative investment
c. Investment performance
d. Asset allocation

8. _____ mature in one year or less. Like zero-coupon bonds, they do not pay interest prior to maturity; instead they are sold at a discount of the par value to create a positive yield to maturity. Many regard _____ as the least risky investment available to U.S. investors.

Chapter 8. Stock Index Futures: Refinements

a. Treasury securities
b. Treasury bills
c. 4-4-5 Calendar
d. Treasury Inflation Protected Securities

9. _____ is a method of hedging a portfolio of stocks against the market risk by short selling stock index futures.

This hedging technique is frequently used by institutional investors when the market direction is uncertain or volatile. Short selling index futures can offset any downturns, but it also hinders any gains.

a. Freight derivative
b. PAUG
c. Delivery month
d. Portfolio insurance

10. A _____ is a private or public market for the trading of company stock and derivatives of company stock at an agreed price; these are securities listed on a stock exchange as well as those only traded privately.

The size of the world _____ is estimated at about $36.6 trillion US at the beginning of October 2008. The world derivatives market has been estimated at about $480 trillion face or nominal value, 12 times the size of the entire world economy.

a. Andrew Tobias
b. Adolph Coors
c. Stock market
d. Anton Gelonkin

11. _____ most frequently refers to the standard deviation of the continuously compounded returns of a financial instrument with a specific time horizon. It is often used to quantify the risk of the instrument over that time period. _____ is typically expressed in annualized terms, and it may either be an absolute number ($5) or a fraction of the mean (5%).

a. Volatility
b. Currency swap
c. Portfolio insurance
d. Seasoned equity offering

12. A _____ is a sudden dramatic decline of stock prices across a significant cross-section of a stock market. Crashes are driven by panic as much as by underlying economic factors. They often follow speculative stock market bubbles.

Chapter 8. Stock Index Futures: Refinements

a. 4-4-5 Calendar
b. 7-Eleven
c. Stock market crash
d. 529 plan

Chapter 9. Foreign Currency Futures

1. A _____, also FX future or foreign exchange future, is a futures contract to exchange one currency for another at a specified date in the future at a price (exchange rate) that is fixed on the purchase date. Typically, one of the currencies is the US dollar. The price of a future is then in terms of US dollars per unit of other currency.

    a. Currency swap
    b. Non-deliverable forward
    c. Foreign exchange controls
    d. Currency future

2. In finance, a _____ is a standardized contract, to buy or sell a specified commodity of standardized quality at a certain date in the future, at a market determined price (the futures price.)

    The price is determined by the instantaneous equilibrium between the forces of supply and demand among competing buy and sell orders on the exchange at the time of the purchase or sale of the contract.

    In many cases, the items may be such non-traditional 'commodities' as foreign currencies, commercial or government paper [e.g., bonds], or 'baskets' of corporate equity ['stock indices'] or other financial instruments.

    a. Financial future
    b. Heston model
    c. Futures contract
    d. Repurchase agreement

3. In economics and finance, _____ is the practice of taking advantage of a price differential between two or more markets: striking a combination of matching deals that capitalize upon the imbalance, the profit being the difference between the market prices. When used by academics, an _____ is a transaction that involves no negative cash flow at any probabilistic or temporal state and a positive cash flow in at least one state; in simple terms, a risk-free profit.

    a. Arbitrage
    b. Initial margin
    c. Issuer
    d. Efficient-market hypothesis

4. _____ are a currency pair that does not include USD, such as GBP/JPY. Pairs that involve the EUR are called euro crosses, such as EUR/GBP. All other currency pairs (those that don't involve USD or EUR) are generally referred to as _____.

    a. Foreign exchange risk
    b. Cross rates
    c. 529 plan
    d. 4-4-5 Calendar

Chapter 9. Foreign Currency Futures

5. _____ is a fee paid on borrowed assets. It is the price paid for the use of borrowed money, or, money earned by deposited funds. Assets that are sometimes lent with _____ include money, shares, consumer goods through hire purchase, major assets such as aircraft, and even entire factories in finance lease arrangements.
   a. Interest
   b. AAB
   c. Insolvency
   d. A Random Walk Down Wall Street

6. An _____ is the price a borrower pays for the use of money they do not own, and the return a lender receives for deferring the use of funds, by lending it to the borrower. _____s are normally expressed as a percentage rate over the period of one year.

   _____s targets are also a vital tool of monetary policy and are used to control variables like investment, inflation, and unemployment.

   a. Interest rate
   b. ABN Amro
   c. A Random Walk Down Wall Street
   d. AAB

7. _____ is an economic concept, expressed as a basic algebraic identity that relates interest rates and exchange rates. The identity is theoretical, and usually follows from assumptions imposed in economics models. There is evidence to support as well as to refute the concept.
   a. AAB
   b. Interest rate parity
   c. Unit price
   d. A Random Walk Down Wall Street

8. _____ refers to a business or organization attempting to acquire goods or services to accomplish the goals of the enterprise. Though there are several organizations that attempt to set standards in the _____ process, processes can vary greatly between organizations. Typically the word '_____' is not used interchangeably with the word 'procurement', since procurement typically includes Expediting, Supplier Quality, and Traffic and Logistics (T'L) in addition to _____.
   a. 529 plan
   b. 7-Eleven
   c. 4-4-5 Calendar
   d. Purchasing

Chapter 9. Foreign Currency Futures

9. _____ is the value of goods/services compared to the amount paid with a currency. Currency can be either a commodity money, like gold or silver, or fiat currency like US dollars which are the world reserve currency. As Adam Smith noted, having money gives one the ability to 'command' others' labor, so _____ to some extent is power over other people, to the extent that they are willing to trade their labor or goods for money or currency.

   a. 4-4-5 Calendar
   b. Purchasing power
   c. 7-Eleven
   d. 529 plan

10. In finance, the _____ between two currencies specifies how much one currency is worth in terms of the other. For example an _____ of 102 Japanese yen to the United States dollar means that JPY 102 is worth the same as USD 1. The foreign exchange market is one of the largest markets in the world.

    a. Exchange rate
    b. ABN Amro
    c. AAB
    d. A Random Walk Down Wall Street

11. A _____, sometimes called a pegged exchange rate, is a type of exchange rate regime wherein a currency's value is matched to the value of another single currency or to a basket of other currencies, or to another measure of value such as gold.

    A _____ is usually used to stabilize the value of a currency, vis-a-vis the currency it is pegged to. This facilitates trade and investments between the two countries, and is especially useful for small economies where external trade forms a large part of their GDP.

    a. Fixed exchange rate
    b. Human capital
    c. Deflation
    d. Market structure

12. The _____ theory uses the long-term equilibrium exchange rate of two currencies to equalize their purchasing power. Developed by Gustav Cassel in 1920, it is based on the law of one price: the theory states that, in ideally efficient markets, identical goods should have only one price.

    This purchasing power SEM rate equalizes the purchasing power of different currencies in their home countries for a given basket of goods.

a. TED spread
b. Gross national product
c. 4-4-5 Calendar
d. Purchasing power parity

13. _____ (in a financial context) is the assumption of the risk of loss, in return for the uncertain possibility of a reward. Only if one may safely say that a particular position involves no risk may one say, strictly speaking, that such a position represents an 'investment.' Financial _____ involves the buying, holding, selling, and short-selling of stocks, bonds, commodities, currencies, collectibles, real estate, derivatives, or any valuable financial instrument to profit from fluctuations in its price as opposed to buying it for use or for income via methods such as dividends or interest. _____ represents one of four market roles in Western financial markets, distinct from hedging, long- or short-term investing, and arbitrage.
a. Forward market
b. Market anomaly
c. Central Securities Depository
d. Speculation

Chapter 10. The Options Market

1. An _____ is a contract written by a seller that conveys to the buyer the right -- but not the obligation -- to buy (in the case of a call _____) or to sell (in the case of a put _____) a particular asset, such as a piece of property such as, among others, a futures contract. In return for granting the _____, the seller collects a payment (the premium) from the buyer.

   For example, buying a call _____ provides the right to buy a specified quantity of a security at a set strike price at some time on or before expiration, while buying a put _____ provides the right to sell.

   a. AT'T Mobility LLC
   b. Annuity
   c. Amortization
   d. Option

2. A _____ is a financial contract between two parties, the buyer and the seller of this type of option. Often it is simply labeled a 'call'. The buyer of the option has the right, but not the obligation to buy an agreed quantity of a particular commodity or financial instrument (the underlying instrument) from the seller of the option at a certain time (the expiration date) for a certain price (the strike price.)

   a. Bear call spread
   b. Call option
   c. Bear spread
   d. Bull spread

3. A _____ is a financial contract between two parties, the seller (writer) and the buyer of the option. The put allows its buyer the right but not the obligation to sell a commodity or financial instrument (the underlying instrument) to the writer (seller) of the option at a certain time for a certain price (the strike price.) The writer (seller) has the obligation to purchase the underlying asset at that strike price, if the buyer exercises the option.

   a. Bear spread
   b. Debit spread
   c. Bear call spread
   d. Put option

4. In finance, _____ is a measure of the degree to which a derivative is likely to have positive monetary value at its expiration, in the risk-neutral measure. It can be measured in percentage probability, or in standard deviations.

   The intrinsic value (or 'monetary value') of an option is the value of exercising it now.

Chapter 10. The Options Market

a. Strike price
b. Bear call spread
c. Moneyness
d. Barrier option

5. A _____ is an exchange of promises between two or more parties to do an act which is enforceable in a court of law. It is where an unqualified offer meets a qualified acceptance and the parties reach Consensus ad Idem. The parties must have the necessary capacity to _____ and the _____ must not be either trifling, indeterminate, impossible or illegal.

a. 4-4-5 Calendar
b. 529 plan
c. 7-Eleven
d. Contract

6. An _____ is defined as 'a promise which meets the requirements for the formation of a contract and limits the promisor's power to revoke an offer.' Restatement (Second) of Contracts § 25 (1981.)

Quite simply, an _____ is a type of contract that protects an offeree from an offeror's ability to revoke the contract.

Consideration for the _____ is still required as it is still a form of contract.

a. AAB
b. A Random Walk Down Wall Street
c. ABN Amro
d. Option contract

7. _____ is a mathematical science pertaining to the collection, analysis, interpretation or explanation, and presentation of data. It also provides tools for prediction and forecasting based on data. It is applicable to a wide variety of academic disciplines, from the natural and social sciences to the humanities, government and business.

a. Mean
b. Sample size
c. Covariance
d. Statistics

8. In finance, a _____ is a standardized contract, to buy or sell a specified commodity of standardized quality at a certain date in the future, at a market determined price (the futures price.)

Chapter 10. The Options Market

The price is determined by the instantaneous equilibrium between the forces of supply and demand among competing buy and sell orders on the exchange at the time of the purchase or sale of the contract.

In many cases, the items may be such non-traditional 'commodities' as foreign currencies, commercial or government paper [e.g., bonds], or 'baskets' of corporate equity ['stock indices'] or other financial instruments.

a. Repurchase agreement
b. Heston model
c. Financial future
d. Futures contract

9. The institution most often referenced by the word '_____' is a public or publicly traded _____, the shares of which are traded on a public stock exchange (e.g., the New York Stock Exchange or Nasdaq in the United States) where shares of stock of _____s are bought and sold by and to the general public. Most of the largest businesses in the world are publicly traded _____s. However, the majority of _____s are said to be closely held, privately held or close _____s, meaning that no ready market exists for the trading of shares.

a. Depository Trust Company
b. Corporation
c. Protect
d. Federal Home Loan Mortgage Corporation

10. A _____ is a firm that quotes both a buy and a sell price in a financial instrument or commodity, hoping to make a profit on the bid/offer spread, or turn.

In foreign exchange trading, where most deals are conducted over-the-counter and are, therefore, completely virtual, the _____ sells to and buys from its clients. Hence, the client's loss and the spread is the _____ firm's profit, which gets thus compensated for the effort of providing liquidity in a competitive market.

a. 7-Eleven
b. 529 plan
c. Market maker
d. 4-4-5 Calendar

11. A _____ is a member of an exchange who is an employee of a member firm and executes orders, as agent, on the floor of the exchange for clients. The _____ receives an order via teletype machine from his firm's trading department and then proceeds to the appropriate trading post on the exchange floor. There he joins other brokers and the specialist in the security being bought or sold and executes the trade at the best competitive price available.

Chapter 10. The Options Market

a. Business valuation standards
b. Multivariate normal distribution
c. Case-Shiller Home Price Indices
d. Floor broker

12. A _____ is a financial services company that provides clearing and settlement services for financial transactions, usually on a futures exchange, and often acts as central counterparty (the payor actually pays the _____, which then pays the payee). A _____ may also offer novation, the substitution of a new contract or debt for an old, or other credit enhancement services to its members.

The term is also used for banks like Suffolk Bank that acted as a restraint on the over-issuance of private bank notes.

a. Valuation
b. Warrant
c. Bucket shop
d. Clearing house

13. In finance, a _____ is collateral that the holder of a position in securities, options, or futures contracts has to deposit to cover the credit risk of his counterparty (most often his broker.) This risk can arise if the holder has done any of the following:

- borrowed cash from the counterparty to buy securities or options,
- sold securities or options short, or
- entered into a futures contract.

The collateral can be in the form of cash or securities, and it is deposited in a _____ account. On U.S. futures exchanges, '_____' was formally called performance bond.

_____ buying is buying securities with cash borrowed from a broker, using other securities as collateral.

a. Credit
b. Share
c. Margin
d. Procter ' Gamble

14. The _____ is the amount required to be collateralized in order to open a position. Thereafter, the amount required to be kept in collateral until the position is closed is the maintenance requirement. The maintenance requirement is the minimum amount to be collateralized in order to keep an open position.

Chapter 10. The Options Market

a. A Random Walk Down Wall Street
b. AAB
c. ABN Amro
d. Initial margin requirement

15. The _____ requirement is the amount required to be collateralized in order to open a position. Thereafter, the amount required to be kept in collateral until the position is closed is the maintenance requirement. The maintenance requirement is the minimum amount to be collateralized in order to keep an open position.

a. Initial margin
b. Arbitrage
c. Efficient-market hypothesis
d. Issuer

16. A _____ occurs when a speculator writes (sells) a call option on a security without ownership of that security. It is one of the riskiest options strategies because it carries unlimited risk as opposed to a naked put where the maximum loss occurs if the stock falls to zero.

The buyer of a call option has the right to buy a specific number of shares at a strike price before an expiration date from the call option seller.

a. Comanity
b. Rate of return
c. Naked call
d. Bed Bath ' Beyond Inc.

Chapter 11. Option Payoffs and Option Strategies

1. An _____ is a contract written by a seller that conveys to the buyer the right -- but not the obligation -- to buy (in the case of a call _____) or to sell (in the case of a put _____) a particular asset, such as a piece of property such as, among others, a futures contract. In return for granting the _____, the seller collects a payment (the premium) from the buyer.

   For example, buying a call _____ provides the right to buy a specified quantity of a security at a set strike price at some time on or before expiration, while buying a put _____ provides the right to sell.

   a. AT'T Mobility LLC
   b. Annuity
   c. Amortization
   d. Option

2. In finance, a _____ is a debt security, in which the authorized issuer owes the holders a debt and, depending on the terms of the _____, is obliged to pay interest (the coupon) and/or to repay the principal at a later date, termed maturity.

   Thus a _____ is a loan: the issuer is the borrower, the _____ holder is the lender, and the coupon is the interest. _____s provide the borrower with external funds to finance long-term investments, or, in the case of government _____s, to finance current expenditure.

   a. Puttable bond
   b. Catastrophe bonds
   c. Bond
   d. Convertible bond

3. In business and finance, a _____ (also referred to as equity _____) of stock means a _____ of ownership in a corporation (company.) In the plural, stocks is often used as a synonym for _____s especially in the United States, but it is less commonly used that way outside of North America.

   In the United Kingdom, South Africa, and Australia, stock can also refer to completely different financial instruments such as government bonds or, less commonly, to all kinds of marketable securities.

   a. Share
   b. Procter ' Gamble
   c. Bucket shop
   d. Margin

Chapter 11. Option Payoffs and Option Strategies

4. A _____ is a financial contract between two parties, the buyer and the seller of this type of option. Often it is simply labeled a 'call'. The buyer of the option has the right, but not the obligation to buy an agreed quantity of a particular commodity or financial instrument (the underlying instrument) from the seller of the option at a certain time (the expiration date) for a certain price (the strike price.)
   a. Bear call spread
   b. Bull spread
   c. Bear spread
   d. Call option

5. In economics and finance, _____ is the practice of taking advantage of a price differential between two or more markets: striking a combination of matching deals that capitalize upon the imbalance, the profit being the difference between the market prices. When used by academics, an _____ is a transaction that involves no negative cash flow at any probabilistic or temporal state and a positive cash flow in at least one state; in simple terms, a risk-free profit.
   a. Initial margin
   b. Efficient-market hypothesis
   c. Issuer
   d. Arbitrage

6. A _____ is a financial contract between two parties, the seller (writer) and the buyer of the option. The put allows its buyer the right but not the obligation to sell a commodity or financial instrument (the underlying instrument) to the writer (seller) of the option at a certain time for a certain price (the strike price.) The writer (seller) has the obligation to purchase the underlying asset at that strike price, if the buyer exercises the option.
   a. Debit spread
   b. Put option
   c. Bear spread
   d. Bear call spread

7. In finance, _____ is a measure of the degree to which a derivative is likely to have positive monetary value at its expiration, in the risk-neutral measure. It can be measured in percentage probability, or in standard deviations.

The intrinsic value (or 'monetary value') of an option is the value of exercising it now.

   a. Strike price
   b. Moneyness
   c. Bear call spread
   d. Barrier option

Chapter 11. Option Payoffs and Option Strategies

8. In finance, a _____ is an investment strategy involving the purchase or sale of particular option derivatives that allows the holder to profit based on how much the price of the underlying security moves, regardless of the direction of price movement. The purchase of particular option derivatives is known as a long _____, while the sale of the option derivatives is known as a short _____.

An option payoff diagram for a long _____ position

A long _____ involves going long, i.e., purchasing, both a call option and a put option on some stock, interest rate, index or other underlying.

   a. Moneyness
   b. Put option
   c. Bear call spread
   d. Straddle

9. _____ is compression of the neck that leads to unconsciousness or death by causing an increasingly hypoxic state in the brain. Fatal _____ typically occurs in cases of violence, accidents, and as the mechanism of suicide in hangings. _____ does not have to be fatal; limited or interrupted _____ is practiced in erotic asphyxia, in the choking game, and is an important technique in many combat sports and self-defense systems

   a. 4-4-5 Calendar
   b. 7-Eleven
   c. 529 plan
   d. Strangling

10. In options trading, a _____ is a bearish, vertical spread options strategy that can be used when the options trader is moderately bearish on the underlying security.

Because of put-call parity, a _____ can be constructed using either put options or call options. If constructed using calls, it is a bear call spread.

   a. Barrier option
   b. Net volatility
   c. Bull spread
   d. Bear spread

11. In options trading, a _____ is a combination of positions that has a certain (i.e. riskless) payoff, considered to be simply 'delta neutral interest rate position'. For example, a bull spread constructed from calls (e.g. long a 50 call, short a 60 call) combined with a bear spread constructed from puts (e.g. long a 60 put, short a 50 put), has a constant payoff of the difference in exercise prices (e.g. 10.) Under the no-arbitrage assumption the net premium paid out to acquire this position should be equal to the present value of the payoff.

Chapter 11. Option Payoffs and Option Strategies

a. Price-to-book ratio
b. Box spread
c. Whisper numbers
d. Stockholder

12. In options trading, a _____ (sometimes simply butterfly) is a combination trade resulting in the following net position:

- Long 1 call at (X − a) strike
- Short 2 calls at X strike
- Long 1 call at (X + a) strike

all with the same expiration date. At expiration the position will be worth zero if the underlying is below X−a or above X+a, and will be worth a positive amount between these two values. The payoff function is shaped like an upside-down V, and the maximum payoff occurs at X

Since the payoff is sometimes zero, sometimes positive, the price of a butterfly is always non-negative (to avoid an arbitrage opportunity.)

a. Long butterfly
b. Naked put
c. Bear spread
d. Binary option

13. A _____ is a transaction in which the seller of call options already owns the corresponding amount of the underlying instrument, such as shares of a stock or other securities. These owned shares provide the 'cover' as they can be handed over to the buyer of the options when he decides to exercise them, instead of having to buy the optioned shares at unfavorable market prices in the case of 'uncovered' or short call. Thus, the _____ limits the (potentially unlimited) loss that results from a short call when the price of the underlying stock moves above the strike price of the option.

a. 529 plan
b. Covered call
c. 7-Eleven
d. 4-4-5 Calendar

14. _____ is a method of hedging a portfolio of stocks against the market risk by short selling stock index futures. This hedging technique is frequently used by institutional investors when the market direction is uncertain or volatile. Short selling index futures can offset any downturns, but it also hinders any gains.

Chapter 11. Option Payoffs and Option Strategies

a. Delivery month
b. PAUG
c. Freight derivative
d. Portfolio insurance

15. In financial mathematics, _____ defines a relationship between the price of a call option and a put option--both with the identical strike price and expiry. To derive the _____ relationship, the assumption is that the options are not exercised before expiration day, which necessarily applies to European options. _____ can be derived in a manner that is largely model independent.

a. Rendleman-Bartter model
b. Hull-White model
c. Cox-Ingersoll-Ross model
d. Put-call parity

Chapter 12. Bounds on Option Prices

1. An _____ is a contract written by a seller that conveys to the buyer the right -- but not the obligation -- to buy (in the case of a call _____) or to sell (in the case of a put _____) a particular asset, such as a piece of property such as, among others, a futures contract. In return for granting the _____, the seller collects a payment (the premium) from the buyer.

   For example, buying a call _____ provides the right to buy a specified quantity of a security at a set strike price at some time on or before expiration, while buying a put _____ provides the right to sell.

   a. AT'T Mobility LLC
   b. Amortization
   c. Option
   d. Annuity

2. A _____ is a financial contract between two parties, the seller (writer) and the buyer of the option. The put allows its buyer the right but not the obligation to sell a commodity or financial instrument (the underlying instrument) to the writer (seller) of the option at a certain time for a certain price (the strike price.) The writer (seller) has the obligation to purchase the underlying asset at that strike price, if the buyer exercises the option.

   a. Debit spread
   b. Bear spread
   c. Bear call spread
   d. Put option

3. A _____ is a financial contract between two parties, the buyer and the seller of this type of option. Often it is simply labeled a 'call'. The buyer of the option has the right, but not the obligation to buy an agreed quantity of a particular commodity or financial instrument (the underlying instrument) from the seller of the option at a certain time (the expiration date) for a certain price (the strike price.)

   a. Bull spread
   b. Call option
   c. Bear call spread
   d. Bear spread

4. In options, the _____ is a key variable in a derivatives contract between two parties. Where the contract requires delivery of the underlying instrument, the trade will be at the _____, regardless of the spot price (market price) of the underlying instrument at that time.

   Definition - The fixed price at which the owner of an option can purchase, in the case of a call in the case of a put, the underlying security or commodity.

Chapter 12. Bounds on Option Prices

a. Swaption
b. Naked put
c. Moneyness
d. Strike price

5. _____ is the value on a given date of a future payment or series of future payments, discounted to reflect the time value of money and other factors such as investment risk. _____ calculations are widely used in business and economics to provide a means to compare cash flows at different times on a meaningful 'like to like' basis.

The most commonly applied model of the time value of money is compound interest.

a. Negative gearing
b. Net present value
c. Present value
d. Present value of benefits

6. A _____ is the price of a single share of a no. of saleable stocks of the company. Once the stock is purchased, the owner becomes a shareholder of the company that issued the share.

a. Stock split
b. Trading curb
c. Whisper numbers
d. Share price

7. In business and finance, a _____ (also referred to as equity _____) of stock means a _____ of ownership in a corporation (company.) In the plural, stocks is often used as a synonym for _____s especially in the United States, but it is less commonly used that way outside of North America.

In the United Kingdom, South Africa, and Australia, stock can also refer to completely different financial instruments such as government bonds or, less commonly, to all kinds of marketable securities.

a. Bucket shop
b. Procter ' Gamble
c. Share
d. Margin

8. _____ is a fee paid on borrowed assets. It is the price paid for the use of borrowed money , or, money earned by deposited funds . Assets that are sometimes lent with _____ include money, shares, consumer goods through hire purchase, major assets such as aircraft, and even entire factories in finance lease arrangements.

Chapter 12. Bounds on Option Prices

a. Insolvency
b. A Random Walk Down Wall Street
c. AAB
d. Interest

9. An _____ is the price a borrower pays for the use of money they do not own, and the return a lender receives for deferring the use of funds, by lending it to the borrower. _____s are normally expressed as a percentage rate over the period of one year.

_____s targets are also a vital tool of monetary policy and are used to control variables like investment, inflation, and unemployment.

a. AAB
b. ABN Amro
c. Interest rate
d. A Random Walk Down Wall Street

10. _____ is a derivative financial instrument.

The global market for exchange-traded _____s is notionally valued by the Bank for International Settlements at $3,075,400 million in 2005.

a. Economic entity
b. Interest rate option
c. Education production function
d. Eurobond

Chapter 13. European Option Pricing

1. An _____ is a contract written by a seller that conveys to the buyer the right -- but not the obligation -- to buy (in the case of a call _____) or to sell (in the case of a put _____) a particular asset, such as a piece of property such as, among others, a futures contract. In return for granting the _____, the seller collects a payment (the premium) from the buyer.

   For example, buying a call _____ provides the right to buy a specified quantity of a security at a set strike price at some time on or before expiration, while buying a put _____ provides the right to sell.

   a. Annuity
   b. Amortization
   c. AT'T Mobility LLC
   d. Option

2. In finance, the binomial options pricing model (BOPM) provides a generalisable numerical method for the valuation of options. The _____ was first proposed by Cox, Ross and Rubinstein (1979.) Essentially, the model uses a 'discrete-time' model of the varying price over time of the underlying financial instrument.
   a. Modified Internal Rate of Return
   b. Perpetuity
   c. Discount rate
   d. Binomial model

3. A _____ is a financial contract between two parties, the seller (writer) and the buyer of the option. The put allows its buyer the right but not the obligation to sell a commodity or financial instrument (the underlying instrument) to the writer (seller) of the option at a certain time for a certain price (the strike price.) The writer (seller) has the obligation to purchase the underlying asset at that strike price, if the buyer exercises the option.
   a. Debit spread
   b. Bear call spread
   c. Bear spread
   d. Put option

4. A _____ is the price of a single share of a no. of saleable stocks of the company. Once the stock is purchased, the owner becomes a shareholder of the company that issued the share.
   a. Stock split
   b. Whisper numbers
   c. Share price
   d. Trading curb

Chapter 13. European Option Pricing

5. The term _____ refers to three closely related concepts:

   - The _____ model is a mathematical model of the market for an equity, in which the equity's price is a stochastic process.
   - The _____ PDE is a partial differential equation which (in the model) must be satisfied by the price of a derivative on the equity.
   - The _____ formula is the result obtained by solving the _____ PDE for a European call option.

   Fischer Black and Myron Scholes first articulated the _____ formula in their 1973 paper, 'The Pricing of Options and Corporate Liabilities.' The foundation for their research relied on work developed by scholars such as Jack L. Treynor, Paul Samuelson, A. James Boness, Sheen T. Kassouf, and Edward O. Thorp. The fundamental insight of _____ is that the option is implicitly priced if the stock is traded.

   Robert C. Merton was the first to publish a paper expanding the mathematical understanding of the options pricing model and coined the term '_____' options pricing model.

   a. Perpetuity
   b. Stochastic volatility
   c. Modified Internal Rate of Return
   d. Black-Scholes

6. A _____ is a financial contract between two parties, the buyer and the seller of this type of option. Often it is simply labeled a 'call'. The buyer of the option has the right, but not the obligation to buy an agreed quantity of a particular commodity or financial instrument (the underlying instrument) from the seller of the option at a certain time (the expiration date) for a certain price (the strike price.)

   a. Bear spread
   b. Bull spread
   c. Bear call spread
   d. Call option

7. _____ is a fee paid on borrowed assets. It is the price paid for the use of borrowed money, or, money earned by deposited funds. Assets that are sometimes lent with _____ include money, shares, consumer goods through hire purchase, major assets such as aircraft, and even entire factories in finance lease arrangements.

   a. Interest
   b. Insolvency
   c. AAB
   d. A Random Walk Down Wall Street

Chapter 13. European Option Pricing

8. In probability and statistics, the _____ of a collection of numbers is a measure of the dispersion of the numbers from their expected (mean) value. It can apply to a probability distribution, a random variable, a population or a data set. The _____ is usually denoted with the letter σ (lowercase sigma.)
   a. Mean
   b. Kurtosis
   c. Sample size
   d. Standard deviation

9. In financial mathematics, the _____ of an option contract is the volatility implied by the market price of the option based on an option pricing model. In other words, it is the volatility that, given a particular pricing model, yields a theoretical value for the option equal to the current market price. Non-option financial instruments that have embedded optionality, such as an interest rate cap, can also have an _____.
   a. Interest rate future
   b. Implied volatility
   c. Interest rate derivative
   d. Equity derivative

10. _____ most frequently refers to the standard deviation of the continuously compounded returns of a financial instrument with a specific time horizon. It is often used to quantify the risk of the instrument over that time period. _____ is typically expressed in annualized terms, and it may either be an absolute number ($5) or a fraction of the mean (5%).
    a. Portfolio insurance
    b. Currency swap
    c. Volatility
    d. Seasoned equity offering

11. A _____ is a payment made by a corporation to its shareholder members. When a corporation earns a profit or surplus, that money can be put to two uses: it can either be re-invested in the business (called retained earnings), or it can be paid to the shareholders as a _____. Many corporations retain a portion of their earnings and pay the remainder as a _____.
    a. Special dividend
    b. Dividend puzzle
    c. Dividend yield
    d. Dividend

12. _____ means regulating, adapting or settling in a variety of contexts:

Chapter 13. European Option Pricing

In commercial law, _____ means the settlement of a loss incurred on insured goods. The calculation of the amounts of compensation to be paid by or to the several interests is a complicated matter. It involves much detail and arithmetic, and requires a full and accurate knowledge of the principles of the subject.

a. Equity method
b. Intelligent investor
c. Asset recovery
d. Adjustment

13. The _____ on a company stock is the company's annual dividend payments divided by its market cap, or the dividend per share divided by the price per share. It is often expressed as a percentage.

Dividend payments on preferred shares are stipulated by the prospectus.

a. Dividend imputation
b. Dividend yield
c. Special dividend
d. Dividend reinvestment plan

14. In finance, the term _____ describes the amount in cash that returns to the owners of a security. Normally it does not include the price variations, at the difference of the total return. _____ applies to various stated rates of return on stocks (common and preferred, and convertible), fixed income instruments (bonds, notes, bills, strips, zero coupon), and some other investment type insurance products (e.g. annuities.)

a. Yield to maturity
b. Yield
c. Macaulay duration
d. 4-4-5 Calendar

Chapter 14. Option Sensitivities and Option Hedging

1. The term _____ refers to three closely related concepts:

   - The _____ model is a mathematical model of the market for an equity, in which the equity's price is a stochastic process.
   - The _____ PDE is a partial differential equation which (in the model) must be satisfied by the price of a derivative on the equity.
   - The _____ formula is the result obtained by solving the _____ PDE for a European call option.

   Fischer Black and Myron Scholes first articulated the _____ formula in their 1973 paper, 'The Pricing of Options and Corporate Liabilities.' The foundation for their research relied on work developed by scholars such as Jack L. Treynor, Paul Samuelson, A. James Boness, Sheen T. Kassouf, and Edward O. Thorp. The fundamental insight of _____ is that the option is implicitly priced if the stock is traded.

   Robert C. Merton was the first to publish a paper expanding the mathematical understanding of the options pricing model and coined the term '_____' options pricing model.

   a. Perpetuity
   b. Modified Internal Rate of Return
   c. Stochastic volatility
   d. Black-Scholes

2. An _____ is a contract written by a seller that conveys to the buyer the right -- but not the obligation -- to buy (in the case of a call _____) or to sell (in the case of a put _____) a particular asset, such as a piece of property such as, among others, a futures contract. In return for granting the _____, the seller collects a payment (the premium) from the buyer.

   For example, buying a call _____ provides the right to buy a specified quantity of a security at a set strike price at some time on or before expiration, while buying a put _____ provides the right to sell.

   a. Annuity
   b. Option
   c. Amortization
   d. AT'T Mobility LLC

3. In finance, a _____ is an investment strategy involving the purchase or sale of particular option derivatives that allows the holder to profit based on how much the price of the underlying security moves, regardless of the direction of price movement. The purchase of particular option derivatives is known as a long _____, while the sale of the option derivatives is known as a short _____.

   An option payoff diagram for a long _____ position

Chapter 14. Option Sensitivities and Option Hedging

A long _____ involves going long, i.e., purchasing, both a call option and a put option on some stock, interest rate, index or other underlying.

a. Straddle
b. Bear call spread
c. Moneyness
d. Put option

4. _____ is compression of the neck that leads to unconsciousness or death by causing an increasingly hypoxic state in the brain. Fatal _____ typically occurs in cases of violence, accidents, and as the mechanism of suicide in hangings. _____ does not have to be fatal; limited or interrupted _____ is practiced in erotic asphyxia, in the choking game, and is an important technique in many combat sports and self-defense systems

a. 7-Eleven
b. Strangling
c. 529 plan
d. 4-4-5 Calendar

5. In options trading, a _____ (sometimes simply butterfly) is a combination trade resulting in the following net position:

- Long 1 call at (X − a) strike
- Short 2 calls at X strike
- Long 1 call at (X + a) strike

all with the same expiration date. At expiration the position will be worth zero if the underlying is below X−a or above X+a, and will be worth a positive amount between these two values. The payoff function is shaped like an upside-down V, and the maximum payoff occurs at X

Since the payoff is sometimes zero, sometimes positive, the price of a butterfly is always non-negative (to avoid an arbitrage opportunity.)

a. Binary option
b. Naked put
c. Long butterfly
d. Bear spread

6. In options trading, a _____ is a bullish, vertical spread options strategy that is designed to profit from a moderate rise in the price of the underlying security.

Chapter 14. Option Sensitivities and Option Hedging

Because of put-call parity, a _____ can be constructed using either put options or call options. If constructed using calls, it is a bull call spread.

a. Bull spread
b. Calendar spread
c. Call option
d. Strike price

7. In finance, a _____ is an option spread trade involving the purchase of options of an underlying market expiring in some named month, and the simultaneous sale of other options of the same underlying market and the same striking price in a different month.

The usual _____, also called a time spread or horizontal spread, involves the purchase of options of a named striking price expiring in a more distant month and the sale of options having the same striking price that expire in a more nearby month.

The _____ is a strategy used by the trader in an attempt to take advantage of a difference in the implied volatilities between two different months' options.

a. Debit spread
b. Binary option
c. Calendar spread
d. Put option

Chapter 15. American Option Pricing

1. An _____ is a contract written by a seller that conveys to the buyer the right -- but not the obligation -- to buy (in the case of a call _____) or to sell (in the case of a put _____) a particular asset, such as a piece of property such as, among others, a futures contract. In return for granting the _____, the seller collects a payment (the premium) from the buyer.

   For example, buying a call _____ provides the right to buy a specified quantity of a security at a set strike price at some time on or before expiration, while buying a put _____ provides the right to sell.

   a. AT'T Mobility LLC
   b. Amortization
   c. Annuity
   d. Option

2. A _____ is a financial contract between two parties, the buyer and the seller of this type of option. Often it is simply labeled a 'call'. The buyer of the option has the right, but not the obligation to buy an agreed quantity of a particular commodity or financial instrument (the underlying instrument) from the seller of the option at a certain time (the expiration date) for a certain price (the strike price.)

   a. Call option
   b. Bear call spread
   c. Bear spread
   d. Bull spread

3. In finance, the binomial options pricing model (BOPM) provides a generalisable numerical method for the valuation of options. The _____ was first proposed by Cox, Ross and Rubinstein (1979.) Essentially, the model uses a 'discrete-time' model of the varying price over time of the underlying financial instrument.

   a. Modified Internal Rate of Return
   b. Perpetuity
   c. Discount rate
   d. Binomial model

4. A _____ is a payment made by a corporation to its shareholder members. When a corporation earns a profit or surplus, that money can be put to two uses: it can either be re-invested in the business (called retained earnings), or it can be paid to the shareholders as a _____. Many corporations retain a portion of their earnings and pay the remainder as a _____.

   a. Dividend yield
   b. Special dividend
   c. Dividend puzzle
   d. Dividend

Chapter 16. Options on Stock Indexes, Foreign Currency, and Futures

1. In finance, the binomial options pricing model (BOPM) provides a generalisable numerical method for the valuation of options. The _____ was first proposed by Cox, Ross and Rubinstein (1979.) Essentially, the model uses a 'discrete-time' model of the varying price over time of the underlying financial instrument.
   a. Perpetuity
   b. Binomial model
   c. Modified Internal Rate of Return
   d. Discount rate

2. An _____ is a contract written by a seller that conveys to the buyer the right -- but not the obligation -- to buy (in the case of a call _____) or to sell (in the case of a put _____) a particular asset, such as a piece of property such as, among others, a futures contract. In return for granting the _____, the seller collects a payment (the premium) from the buyer.

   For example, buying a call _____ provides the right to buy a specified quantity of a security at a set strike price at some time on or before expiration, while buying a put _____ provides the right to sell.

   a. Annuity
   b. AT'T Mobility LLC
   c. Amortization
   d. Option

3. A _____ is a method of measuring a section of the stock market. Many indices are cited by news or financial services firms and are used to benchmark the performance of portfolios such as mutual funds.
   a. Stop order
   b. Program trading
   c. Trading curb
   d. Stock market index

4. In finance, a _____ is a standardized contract, to buy or sell a specified commodity of standardized quality at a certain date in the future, at a market determined price (the futures price.)

   The price is determined by the instantaneous equilibrium between the forces of supply and demand among competing buy and sell orders on the exchange at the time of the purchase or sale of the contract.

   In many cases, the items may be such non-traditional 'commodities' as foreign currencies, commercial or government paper [e.g., bonds], or 'baskets' of corporate equity ['stock indices'] or other financial instruments.

a. Repurchase agreement
b. Financial future
c. Heston model
d. Futures contract

5. A _____ is a payment made by a corporation to its shareholder members. When a corporation earns a profit or surplus, that money can be put to two uses: it can either be re-invested in the business (called retained earnings), or it can be paid to the shareholders as a _____. Many corporations retain a portion of their earnings and pay the remainder as a _____.

a. Dividend
b. Dividend yield
c. Dividend puzzle
d. Special dividend

Chapter 17. The Options Approach to Corporate Securities

1. In finance, a _____ is a security that entitles the holder to buy stock of the company that issued it at a specified price, which is usually higher than the stock price at time of issue.

   _____s are frequently attached to bonds or preferred stock as a sweetener, allowing the issuer to pay lower interest rates or dividends. They can be used to enhance the yield of the bond, and make them more attractive to potential buyers.

   a. Clearing house
   b. Credit
   c. Clearing
   d. Warrant

2. An _____ is a contract written by a seller that conveys to the buyer the right -- but not the obligation -- to buy (in the case of a call _____) or to sell (in the case of a put _____) a particular asset, such as a piece of property such as, among others, a futures contract. In return for granting the _____, the seller collects a payment (the premium) from the buyer.

   For example, buying a call _____ provides the right to buy a specified quantity of a security at a set strike price at some time on or before expiration, while buying a put _____ provides the right to sell.

   a. Option
   b. AT'T Mobility LLC
   c. Amortization
   d. Annuity

3. A _____ is a fungible, negotiable instrument representing financial value. They are broadly categorized into debt securities (such as banknotes, bonds and debentures), and equity securities; e.g., common stocks. The company or other entity issuing the _____ is called the issuer.

   a. Tracking stock
   b. Security
   c. Securities lending
   d. Book entry

4. In finance, a _____ is a debt security, in which the authorized issuer owes the holders a debt and, depending on the terms of the _____, is obliged to pay interest (the coupon) and/or to repay the principal at a later date, termed maturity.

   Thus a _____ is a loan: the issuer is the borrower, the _____ holder is the lender, and the coupon is the interest. _____s provide the borrower with external funds to finance long-term investments, or, in the case of government _____s, to finance current expenditure.

Chapter 17. The Options Approach to Corporate Securities

a. Catastrophe bonds
b. Convertible bond
c. Puttable bond
d. Bond

5. A _____ is a financial contract between two parties, the buyer and the seller of this type of option. Often it is simply labeled a 'call'. The buyer of the option has the right, but not the obligation to buy an agreed quantity of a particular commodity or financial instrument (the underlying instrument) from the seller of the option at a certain time (the expiration date) for a certain price (the strike price.)

a. Call option
b. Bear spread
c. Bear call spread
d. Bull spread

6. _____ is a form of corporation equity ownership represented in the securities. It is dangerous in comparison to preferred shares and some other investment options, in that in the event of bankruptcy, _____ investors receive their funds after preferred stockholders, bondholders, creditors, etc. On the other hand, common shares on average perform better than preferred shares or bonds over time.

a. Stock market bubble
b. Stop-limit order
c. Stock split
d. Common stock

7. A '_____' is a 'Charge' that is paid to obtain the right to delay a payment. Essentially, the payer purchases the right to make a given payment in the future instead of in the Present. The '_____', or 'Charge' that must be paid to delay the payment, is simply the difference between what the payment amount would be if it were paid in the present and what the payment amount would be paid if it were paid in the future.

a. Discount
b. Risk modeling
c. Risk aversion
d. Value at risk

8. A _____ is a bond bought at a price lower than its face value, with the face value repaid at the time of maturity. It does not make periodic interest payments, or so-called 'coupons,' hence the term zero-coupon bond. Investors earn return from the compounded interest all paid at maturity plus the difference between the discounted price of the bond and its par value.

Chapter 17. The Options Approach to Corporate Securities

a. Zero coupon bond
b. Municipal bond
c. Callable bond
d. Bowie bonds

9. _____ is that which is owed; usually referencing assets owed, but the term can cover other obligations. In the case of assets, _____ is a means of using future purchasing power in the present before a summation has been earned. Some companies and corporations use _____ as a part of their overall corporate finance strategy.

a. Partial Payment
b. Cross-collateralization
c. Debt
d. Credit cycle

10. In finance, _____ is debt which ranks after other debts should a company fall into receivership or be closed. Such debt is referred to as subordinate, because the debt providers have subordinate status in relationship to the normal debt. A typical example for this would be when a promoter of a company invests money in the form of debt, rather than in the form of stock.

a. Subordinated debt
b. Credit rating
c. Cross-collateralization
d. Participation loan

11. _____ is a type of bond that allows the issuer of the bond to retain the privilege of redeeming the bond at some point before the bond reaches the date of maturity. In other words, on the call dates, the issuer has the right, but not the obligation, to buy back the bonds from the bond holders at the call price. Technically speaking, the bonds are not really bought and held by the issuer but cancelled immediately.

a. Bond fund
b. Gilts
c. Coupon rate
d. Callable bond

12. In finance, a _____ is a type of bond that can be converted into shares of stock in the issuing company, usually at some pre-announced ratio. It is a hybrid security with debt- and equity-like features. Although it typically has a low coupon rate, the holder is compensated with the ability to convert the bond to common stock, usually at a substantial discount to the stock's market value.

a. Corporate bond
b. Convertible bond
c. Bond fund
d. Gilts

Chapter 18. Exotic Options

1. An _____ is a contract written by a seller that conveys to the buyer the right -- but not the obligation -- to buy (in the case of a call _____) or to sell (in the case of a put _____) a particular asset, such as a piece of property such as, among others, a futures contract. In return for granting the _____, the seller collects a payment (the premium) from the buyer.

   For example, buying a call _____ provides the right to buy a specified quantity of a security at a set strike price at some time on or before expiration, while buying a put _____ provides the right to sell.

   a. Option
   b. Amortization
   c. AT'T Mobility LLC
   d. Annuity

2. In finance, a _____ is a type of financial option where the option to exercise depends on the underlying crossing or reaching a given barrier level. _____s were created to provide the insurance value of an option without charging as much premium. For example, if you believe that IBM will go up this year, but are willing to bet that it won't go above $100, then you can buy the barrier and pay less premium than the vanilla option.

   a. Net volatility
   b. Barrier option
   c. Binary option
   d. Naked put

3. In finance, a _____ is a type of option where the payoff is either some fixed amount of some asset or nothing at all. The two main types of _____s are the cash-or-nothing _____ and the asset-or-nothing _____. The cash-or-nothing _____ pays some fixed amount of cash if the option expires in-the-money while the asset-or-nothing pays the value of the underlying security.

   a. Naked put
   b. Calendar spread
   c. Moneyness
   d. Binary option

4. The _____ are a type of exotic options with path dependency, among many other kind of options. The payoff depends on the optimal (maximum or minimum) underlying asset's price occurring over the life of the option. The option allows the holder to 'look back' over time to determine the payoff.

   a. Database auditing
   b. Help desk and incident reporting auditing
   c. Weighted mean
   d. Lookback options

Chapter 18. Exotic Options

5. An _____ (or average value option) is a special type of option contract. For _____s the payoff is determined by the average underlying price over some pre-set period of time. This is different to the case of the usual European option, where the payoff of the option contract depends on the price of the underlying instrument at maturity.

   a. Options arbitrage
   b. Option screener
   c. Options spreads
   d. Asian option

6. In business and accounting, _____s are everything of value that is owned by a person or company. The balance sheet of a firm records the monetary value of the _____s owned by the firm. The two major _____ classes are tangible _____s and intangible _____s.

   a. Income
   b. Accounts payable
   c. EBITDA
   d. Asset

Chapter 19. Interest Rate Options

1. _____ is a fee paid on borrowed assets. It is the price paid for the use of borrowed money, or, money earned by deposited funds. Assets that are sometimes lent with _____ include money, shares, consumer goods through hire purchase, major assets such as aircraft, and even entire factories in finance lease arrangements.
   a. A Random Walk Down Wall Street
   b. Insolvency
   c. AAB
   d. Interest

2. An _____ is the price a borrower pays for the use of money they do not own, and the return a lender receives for deferring the use of funds, by lending it to the borrower. _____s are normally expressed as a percentage rate over the period of one year.

   _____s targets are also a vital tool of monetary policy and are used to control variables like investment, inflation, and unemployment.

   a. ABN Amro
   b. A Random Walk Down Wall Street
   c. AAB
   d. Interest rate

3. _____ is a derivative financial instrument.

   The global market for exchange-traded _____s is notionally valued by the Bank for International Settlements at $3,075,400 million in 2005.

   a. Eurobond
   b. Education production function
   c. Economic entity
   d. Interest rate option

4. An _____ is a contract written by a seller that conveys to the buyer the right -- but not the obligation -- to buy (in the case of a call _____) or to sell (in the case of a put _____) a particular asset, such as a piece of property such as, among others, a futures contract. In return for granting the _____, the seller collects a payment (the premium) from the buyer.

   For example, buying a call _____ provides the right to buy a specified quantity of a security at a set strike price at some time on or before expiration, while buying a put _____ provides the right to sell.

Chapter 19. Interest Rate Options

a. Annuity
b. AT'T Mobility LLC
c. Amortization
d. Option

5. The _____ is a variant of the Black-Scholes option pricing model. Its primary applications are for pricing bond options, interest rate caps / floors, and swaptions. It was first presented in a paper written by Fischer Black in 1976.

The Black formula is similar to the Black-Scholes formula for valuing stock options except that the spot price of the underlying is replaced by the forward price F.

The Black formula for a European call option on an underlying strike at K, expiring T years in the future is

$$c = e^{-rT}[FN(d_1) - KN(d_2)]$$

a. Black model
b. Multivariate normal distribution
c. Fama-French three factor model
d. Moving average

6. A _____ is an asset-backed security whose cash flows are backed by the principal and interest payments of a set of mortgage loans. Payments are typically made monthly over the lifetime of the underlying loans.

a. Home equity line of credit
b. Mortgage-backed security
c. Conforming loan
d. Shared appreciation mortgage

7. A _____ is a financial debt vehicle that was first created in June 1983 by investment banks Salomon Brothers and First Boston for Freddie Mac. (The First Boston team was led by Dexter Senft.) Legally, a _____ is a special purpose entity that is wholly separate from the institution(s) that create it.

a. Tranche
b. Collateralized mortgage obligation
c. 4-4-5 Calendar
d. Yield curve spread

Chapter 19. Interest Rate Options

8. A _____ is a fungible, negotiable instrument representing financial value. They are broadly categorized into debt securities (such as banknotes, bonds and debentures), and equity securities; e.g., common stocks. The company or other entity issuing the _____ is called the issuer.
   a. Tracking stock
   b. Book entry
   c. Securities lending
   d. Security

9. In finance, the yield curve is the relation between the interest rate (or cost of borrowing) and the time to maturity of the debt for a given borrower in a given currency. For example, the current U.S. dollar interest rates paid on U.S. Treasury securities for various maturities are closely watched by many traders, and are commonly plotted on a graph such as the one on the right which is informally called 'the yield curve.' More formal mathematical descriptions of this relation are often called the _____.

   The yield of a debt instrument is the annualized percentage increase in the value of the investment.

   a. 4-4-5 Calendar
   b. 529 plan
   c. 7-Eleven
   d. Term structure of interest rates

10. In finance, the term _____ describes the amount in cash that returns to the owners of a security. Normally it does not include the price variations, at the difference of the total return. _____ applies to various stated rates of return on stocks (common and preferred, and convertible), fixed income instruments (bonds, notes, bills, strips, zero coupon), and some other investment type insurance products (e.g. annuities.)
    a. 4-4-5 Calendar
    b. Yield
    c. Macaulay duration
    d. Yield to maturity

11. In finance, the _____ is the relation between the interest rate (or cost of borrowing) and the time to maturity of the debt for a given borrower in a given currency. For example, the current U.S. dollar interest rates paid on U.S. Treasury securities for various maturities are closely watched by many traders, and are commonly plotted on a graph such as the one on the right which is informally called 'the _____.' More formal mathematical descriptions of this relation are often called the term structure of interest rates.

    The yield of a debt instrument is the annualized percentage increase in the value of the investment.

Chapter 19. Interest Rate Options

a. 7-Eleven
b. 4-4-5 Calendar
c. 529 plan
d. Yield curve

12. The _____ or forward rate is the agreed upon price of an asset in a forward contract. Using the rational pricing assumption, we can express the _____ in terms of the spot price and any dividends etc., so that there is no possibility for arbitrage.

The _____ is given by:

$$F = S_0 e^{(r-q)T} - \sum_i D_i e^{(r-q)(T-t_i)}$$

where

F is the _____ to be paid at time T
e^x is the exponential function
r is the risk-free interest rate
q is the cost-of-carry
S_0 is the spot price of the asset (i.e. what it would sell for at time 0)
D_i is a dividend which is guaranteed to be paid at time t_i where $0 < t_i < T$.

The two questions here are what price the short position (the seller of the asset) should offer to maximize his gain, and what price the long position (the buyer of the asset) should accept to maximize his gain?

At the very least we know that both do not want to lose any money in the deal.

a. Biweekly Mortgage
b. Security interest
c. Forward price
d. Financial Gerontology

13. A _____ is a bond bought at a price lower than its face value, with the face value repaid at the time of maturity. It does not make periodic interest payments, or have so-called 'coupons,' hence the term _____. Investors earn return from the compounded interest all paid at maturity plus the difference between the discounted price of the bond and its par value.

Chapter 19. Interest Rate Options

a. Clean price
b. Corporate bond
c. Zero-coupon bond
d. Bond fund

14. _____ is a method for constructing a (zero-coupon) fixed-income yield curve from the prices of a set of coupon-bearing products by forward substitution.

Using these zero-coupon products it becomes possible to derive par swap rates (forward and spot) for all maturities by making a few assumptions (including linear interpolation.) The term structure of spot returns is recovered from the bond yields by solving for them recursively, this iterative process is called the BootStrap Method.

a. Bootstrapping
b. Probability of default
c. Reserve requirement
d. Bullet loan

15. In finance, a _____ is a forward contract in which one party pays a fixed interest rate, and receives a floating interest rate equal to a reference rate (the underlying rate.) The payments are calculated over a notional amount over a certain period, and netted, i.e. only the differential is paid. It is paid on the effective date.

a. Triple witching hour
b. Local volatility
c. PAUG
d. Forward Rate Agreement

16. _____ are government bonds issued by the United States Department of the Treasury through the Bureau of the Public Debt. They are the debt financing instruments of the U.S. Federal government, and they are often referred to simply as Treasuries or Treasurys. There are four types of marketable _____: Treasury bills, Treasury notes, Treasury bonds, and Treasury Inflation Protected Securities (TIPS.)

a. 4-4-5 Calendar
b. Treasury securities
c. Treasury Inflation Protected Securities
d. Treasury Inflation-Protected Securities

17. _____ is the flat spread over the treasury yield curve required to discount a security payment to match its market price. This concept can be applied to mortgage-backed security (MBS), Options, Bonds and any other interest-rate Derivative.

Chapter 19. Interest Rate Options

In contrast to the simple 'yield curve spread' measurement of bond premium over a pre-determined cash-flow model, the _____ describes the market premium over a model including two types of volatility:

- Variable interest rates
- Variable prepayment rates.

Designing such models in the first place is complicated because prepayment variations are a behavioural function of the stochastic interest rate. (They tend to go up as interest rates come down.)

a. A Random Walk Down Wall Street
b. ABN Amro
c. Option adjusted spread
d. AAB

18. In finance, a _____ is a standardized contract, to buy or sell a specified commodity of standardized quality at a certain date in the future, at a market determined price (the futures price.)

The price is determined by the instantaneous equilibrium between the forces of supply and demand among competing buy and sell orders on the exchange at the time of the purchase or sale of the contract.

In many cases, the items may be such non-traditional 'commodities' as foreign currencies, commercial or government paper [e.g., bonds], or 'baskets' of corporate equity ['stock indices'] or other financial instruments.

a. Financial future
b. Heston model
c. Repurchase agreement
d. Futures contract

19. In finance, a _____ is a debt security, in which the authorized issuer owes the holders a debt and, depending on the terms of the _____, is obliged to pay interest (the coupon) and/or to repay the principal at a later date, termed maturity.

Thus a _____ is a loan: the issuer is the borrower, the _____ holder is the lender, and the coupon is the interest. _____s provide the borrower with external funds to finance long-term investments, or, in the case of government _____s, to finance current expenditure.

a. Puttable bond
b. Catastrophe bonds
c. Convertible bond
d. Bond

20. In finance, a _____ is an OTC-traded financial instrument that facilitates an option to buy or sell a particular bond at a certain date for a particular price. It is similar to a stock option with the difference that the underlying asset is a bond. _____s can be valued using the Black model.
a. Municipal bond
b. Nominal yield
c. Dirty price
d. Bond option

21. In finance, _____ is the interest that has accumulated since the principal investment, or since the previous interest payment if there has been one already. For a financial instrument such as a bond, interest is calculated and paid in set intervals.

The primary formula for calculating the interest accrued in a given period is:

$$I_A = T \times P \times R$$

where I_A is the _____, T is the fraction of the year, P is the principal, and R is the annualized interest rate.

a. AAB
b. A Random Walk Down Wall Street
c. Accrued interest
d. ABN Amro

22. The coupon or _____ of a bond is the amount of interest paid per year expressed as a percentage of the face value of the bond.

For example if you hold $10,000 nominal of a bond described as a 4.5% loan stock, you will receive $450 in interest each year (probably in two installments of $225 each.)

Not all bonds have coupons.

Chapter 19. Interest Rate Options

a. Puttable bond
b. Coupon rate
c. Revenue bonds
d. Zero-coupon bond

23. _____ most frequently refers to the standard deviation of the continuously compounded returns of a financial instrument with a specific time horizon. It is often used to quantify the risk of the instrument over that time period. _____ is typically expressed in annualized terms, and it may either be an absolute number ($5) or a fraction of the mean (5%).

a. Volatility
b. Currency swap
c. Portfolio insurance
d. Seasoned equity offering

24. _____ is a legal term for a type of debt which is overdue after missing an expected payment. It is also used (in the form in _____) for payments that occur at the end of a period.

_____ accrue from the date on the first missed payment was due.

a. A Random Walk Down Wall Street
b. AAB
c. Interest
d. Arrears

25. In financial mathematics, _____ defines a relationship between the price of a call option and a put option--both with the identical strike price and expiry. To derive the _____ relationship, the assumption is that the options are not exercised before expiration day, which necessarily applies to European options. _____ can be derived in a manner that is largely model independent.

a. Put-call parity
b. Cox-Ingersoll-Ross model
c. Rendleman-Bartter model
d. Hull-White model

Chapter 20. The Swaps Market: Introduction

85

1. In finance, a _____ is a derivative in which two counterparties agree to exchange one stream of cash flows against another stream. These streams are called the legs of the _____.

   The cash flows are calculated over a notional principal amount, which is usually not exchanged between counterparties.

   a. Volatility swap
   b. Local volatility
   c. Volatility arbitrage
   d. Swap

2. _____ is a fee paid on borrowed assets. It is the price paid for the use of borrowed money, or, money earned by deposited funds. Assets that are sometimes lent with _____ include money, shares, consumer goods through hire purchase, major assets such as aircraft, and even entire factories in finance lease arrangements.

   a. Insolvency
   b. AAB
   c. A Random Walk Down Wall Street
   d. Interest

3. An _____ is the price a borrower pays for the use of money they do not own, and the return a lender receives for deferring the use of funds, by lending it to the borrower. _____s are normally expressed as a percentage rate over the period of one year.

   _____s targets are also a vital tool of monetary policy and are used to control variables like investment, inflation, and unemployment.

   a. Interest rate
   b. ABN Amro
   c. A Random Walk Down Wall Street
   d. AAB

4. An _____ is a derivative in which one party exchanges a stream of interest payments for another party's stream of cash flows. _____s can be used by hedgers to manage their fixed or floating assets and liabilities. They can also be used by speculators to replicate unfunded bond exposures to profit from changes in interest rates.

   a. Interest rate swap
   b. Implied volatility
   c. Equity swap
   d. International Swaps and Derivatives Association

Chapter 20. The Swaps Market: Introduction

5. A _____ is a foreign exchange agreement between two parties to exchange principal and fixed rate interest payments on a loan in one currency for principal and fixed rate interest payments on an equal (regarding net present value) loan in another currency. They are motivated by comparative advantage.
    a. Currency pair
    b. Currency swap
    c. Forex swap
    d. Foreign exchange market

6. In economics, _____ refers to the ability of a person or a country to produce a particular good at a lower marginal cost and opportunity cost than another person or country. It is the ability to produce a product most efficiently given all the other products that could be produced. It can be contrasted with absolute advantage which refers to the ability of a person or a country to produce a particular good at a lower absolute cost than another.
    a. Reputational risk
    b. Case-Shiller Home Price Indices
    c. Loans and interest, in Judaism
    d. Comparative advantage

7. In business and accounting, _____s are everything of value that is owned by a person or company. The balance sheet of a firm records the monetary value of the _____s owned by the firm. The two major _____ classes are tangible _____s and intangible _____s.
    a. EBITDA
    b. Income
    c. Accounts payable
    d. Asset

8. An _____ is an exchange of tangible assets for intangible assets or vice versa. Since it is a swap of assets, the procedure takes place on the active side of the balance sheet and has no impact on the latter in regards to volume. As an example, a company may sell equity and receive the value in cash thus increasing liquidity.
    a. ABN Amro
    b. AAB
    c. A Random Walk Down Wall Street
    d. Asset Swap

9. _____ is that which is owed; usually referencing assets owed, but the term can cover other obligations. In the case of assets, _____ is a means of using future purchasing power in the present before a summation has been earned. Some companies and corporations use _____ as a part of their overall corporate finance strategy.

Chapter 20. The Swaps Market: Introduction

a. Credit cycle
b. Debt
c. Partial Payment
d. Cross-collateralization

10. _____ in finance is the risk associated with imperfect hedging using futures. It could arise because of the difference between the asset whose price is to be hedged and the asset underlying the derivative, or because of a mismatch between the expiration date of the futures and the actual selling date of the asset.

Under these conditions, the spot price of the asset, and the futures price, do not converge on the expiration date of the future.

a. Liquidity risk
b. Credit risk
c. Currency risk
d. Basis risk

11. A _____ is an institution, firm or individual who mediates between two or more parties in a financial context. Typically the first party is a provider of a product or service and the second party is a consumer or customer.

In the U.S., a _____ is typically an institution that facilitates the channelling of funds between lenders and borrowers indirectly.

a. Financial intermediary
b. Mutual fund
c. Savings and loan association
d. Net asset value

12. _____ is the risk (variability in value) borne by an interest-bearing asset, such as a loan or a bond, due to variability of interest rates. In general, as rates rise, the price of a fixed rate bond will fall, and vice versa. _____ is commonly measured by the bond's duration.

a. A Random Walk Down Wall Street
b. Interest rate risk
c. Official bank rate
d. International Fisher effect

13. A _____ is an interest rate swap which involves the exchange of two floating rate financial instruments. A floating-floating interest rate swap under which the floating rate payments is referenced to different bases.

Chapter 20. The Swaps Market: Introduction

Basis risk occurs for positions that have at least one paying and one receiving stream of cash flows that are driven by different factors and the correlation between those factors are less than one.

a. Creditor
b. Trade date
c. Basis swap
d. Carrying charge

14. In finance, the term _____ describes the amount in cash that returns to the owners of a security. Normally it does not include the price variations, at the difference of the total return. _____ applies to various stated rates of return on stocks (common and preferred, and convertible), fixed income instruments (bonds, notes, bills, strips, zero coupon), and some other investment type insurance products (e.g. annuities.)

a. Yield to maturity
b. Yield
c. 4-4-5 Calendar
d. Macaulay duration

15. In finance, the _____ is the relation between the interest rate (or cost of borrowing) and the time to maturity of the debt for a given borrower in a given currency. For example, the current U.S. dollar interest rates paid on U.S. Treasury securities for various maturities are closely watched by many traders, and are commonly plotted on a graph such as the one on the right which is informally called 'the _____.' More formal mathematical descriptions of this relation are often called the term structure of interest rates.

The yield of a debt instrument is the annualized percentage increase in the value of the investment.

a. 4-4-5 Calendar
b. 7-Eleven
c. Yield curve
d. 529 plan

16. A _____ is something for which there is demand, but which is supplied without qualitative differentiation across a market. It is a product that is the same no matter who produces it, such as petroleum, notebook paper, or milk. In other words, copper is copper.

a. 529 plan
b. Commodity
c. 4-4-5 Calendar
d. 7-Eleven

Chapter 20. The Swaps Market: Introduction

17. An _____ is a swap where a set of future cash flows are exchanged between two counterparties. The two cash flows are usually referred to as 'legs'. One of these cash flow streams can be pegged to floating rate of interest or pay a fixed rate
    a. Equity swap
    b. Interest rate swap
    c. Interest rate derivative
    d. Interest rate future

18. A _____ is an option granting its owner the right but not the obligation to enter into an underlying swap. Although options can be traded on a variety of swaps, the term '_____' typically refers to options on interest rate swaps.

    There are two types of _____ contracts:

    - A payer _____ gives the owner of the _____ the right to enter into a swap where they pay the fixed leg and receive the floating leg.
    - A receiver _____ gives the owner of the _____ the right to enter into a swap where they will receive the fixed leg, and pay the floating leg.

    The buyer and seller of the _____ agree on:

    - the premium (price) of the _____
    - the strike rate (equal to the fixed rate of the underlying swap)
    - length of the option period (which usually ends two business days prior to the start date of the underlying swap),
    - the term of the underlying swap,
    - notional amount,
    - amortization, if any
    - frequency of settlement of payments on the underlying swap

    The participants in the _____ market are predominantly large corporations, banks, financial institutions and hedge funds. End users such as corporations and banks typically use _____s to manage interest rate risk arising from their core business or from their financing arrangements.

    a. Bear call spread
    b. Put option
    c. Swaption
    d. Straddle

Chapter 21. Swaps: Economic Analysis and Pricing

1. In finance, a _____ is a derivative in which two counterparties agree to exchange one stream of cash flows against another stream. These streams are called the legs of the _____.

   The cash flows are calculated over a notional principal amount, which is usually not exchanged between counterparties.

   a. Volatility arbitrage
   b. Local volatility
   c. Volatility swap
   d. Swap

2. The _____ is the market for securities, where companies and governments can raise longterm funds. The _____ includes the stock market and the bond market. Financial regulators, such as the U.S. Securities and Exchange Commission, oversee the _____s in their designated countries to ensure that investors are protected against fraud.

   a. Forward market
   b. Delta neutral
   c. Capital market
   d. Spot rate

3. A _____ is a foreign exchange agreement between two parties to exchange principal and fixed rate interest payments on a loan in one currency for principal and fixed rate interest payments on an equal (regarding net present value) loan in another currency. They are motivated by comparative advantage.

   a. Forex swap
   b. Currency swap
   c. Foreign exchange market
   d. Currency pair

4. _____ is a fee paid on borrowed assets. It is the price paid for the use of borrowed money, or, money earned by deposited funds. Assets that are sometimes lent with _____ include money, shares, consumer goods through hire purchase, major assets such as aircraft, and even entire factories in finance lease arrangements.

   a. AAB
   b. A Random Walk Down Wall Street
   c. Insolvency
   d. Interest

5. An _____ is the price a borrower pays for the use of money they do not own, and the return a lender receives for deferring the use of funds, by lending it to the borrower. _____s are normally expressed as a percentage rate over the period of one year.

Chapter 21. Swaps: Economic Analysis and Pricing

_____s targets are also a vital tool of monetary policy and are used to control variables like investment, inflation, and unemployment.

a. ABN Amro
b. A Random Walk Down Wall Street
c. AAB
d. Interest rate

6. An _____ is a derivative in which one party exchanges a stream of interest payments for another party's stream of cash flows. _____s can be used by hedgers to manage their fixed or floating assets and liabilities. They can also be used by speculators to replicate unfunded bond exposures to profit from changes in interest rates.

a. Equity swap
b. International Swaps and Derivatives Association
c. Implied volatility
d. Interest rate swap

7. The _____ or forward rate is the agreed upon price of an asset in a forward contract. Using the rational pricing assumption, we can express the _____ in terms of the spot price and any dividends etc., so that there is no possibility for arbitrage.

The _____ is given by:

$$\boxed{x}$$

where

F is the _____ to be paid at time T
e^x is the exponential function
r is the risk-free interest rate
q is the cost-of-carry
S_0 is the spot price of the asset (i.e. what it would sell for at time 0)
D_i is a dividend which is guaranteed to be paid at time t_i where $0 < t_i < T$.

The two questions here are what price the short position (the seller of the asset) should offer to maximize his gain, and what price the long position (the buyer of the asset) should accept to maximize his gain?

At the very least we know that both do not want to lose any money in the deal.

Chapter 21. Swaps: Economic Analysis and Pricing

a. Financial Gerontology
b. Forward price
c. Biweekly Mortgage
d. Security interest

8. In finance, a _____ is a forward contract in which one party pays a fixed interest rate, and receives a floating interest rate equal to a reference rate (the underlying rate.) The payments are calculated over a notional amount over a certain period, and netted, i.e. only the differential is paid. It is paid on the effective date.

a. Triple witching hour
b. PAUG
c. Local volatility
d. Forward rate agreement

9. _____ is an economic concept, expressed as a basic algebraic identity that relates interest rates and exchange rates. The identity is theoretical, and usually follows from assumptions imposed in economics models. There is evidence to support as well as to refute the concept.

a. Interest rate parity
b. A Random Walk Down Wall Street
c. AAB
d. Unit price

10. A _____ is an exchange of promises between two or more parties to do an act which is enforceable in a court of law. It is where an unqualified offer meets a qualified acceptance and the parties reach Consensus ad Idem. The parties must have the necessary capacity to _____ and the _____ must not be either trifling, indeterminate, impossible or illegal.

a. 7-Eleven
b. Contract
c. 4-4-5 Calendar
d. 529 plan

11. A _____ is an agreement between two parties to buy or sell an asset at a specified point of time in the future. The price of the underlying instrument, in whatever form, is paid before control of the instrument changes. This is one of the many forms of buy/sell orders where the time of trade is not the time where the securities themselves are exchanged.

Chapter 21. Swaps: Economic Analysis and Pricing

a. Derivatives markets
b. Loan Credit Default Swap Index
c. Forward contract
d. Constant maturity credit default swap

12. _____s are deposits denominated in United States dollars at banks outside the United States, and thus are not under the jurisdiction of the Federal Reserve. Consequently, such deposits are subject to much less regulation than similar deposits within the United States, allowing for higher margins. There is nothing 'European' about _____ deposits; a US dollar-denominated deposit in Tokyo or Caracas would likewise be deemed _____ deposits.

a. ABN Amro
b. Eurodollar
c. A Random Walk Down Wall Street
d. AAB

13. In finance, a _____ is a standardized contract, to buy or sell a specified commodity of standardized quality at a certain date in the future, at a market determined price (the futures price.)

The price is determined by the instantaneous equilibrium between the forces of supply and demand among competing buy and sell orders on the exchange at the time of the purchase or sale of the contract.

In many cases, the items may be such non-traditional 'commodities' as foreign currencies, commercial or government paper [e.g., bonds], or 'baskets' of corporate equity ['stock indices'] or other financial instruments.

a. Heston model
b. Repurchase agreement
c. Financial future
d. Futures contract

14. _____ is a derivative financial instrument.

The global market for exchange-traded _____s is notionally valued by the Bank for International Settlements at $3,075,400 million in 2005.

a. Economic entity
b. Eurobond
c. Education production function
d. Interest rate option

Chapter 21. Swaps: Economic Analysis and Pricing

15. An _____ is a contract written by a seller that conveys to the buyer the right -- but not the obligation -- to buy (in the case of a call _____) or to sell (in the case of a put _____) a particular asset, such as a piece of property such as, among others, a futures contract. In return for granting the _____, the seller collects a payment (the premium) from the buyer.

For example, buying a call _____ provides the right to buy a specified quantity of a security at a set strike price at some time on or before expiration, while buying a put _____ provides the right to sell.

    a. Annuity
    b. Option
    c. AT'T Mobility LLC
    d. Amortization

16. The _____ is a variant of the Black-Scholes option pricing model. Its primary applications are for pricing bond options, interest rate caps / floors, and swaptions. It was first presented in a paper written by Fischer Black in 1976.

The Black formula is similar to the Black-Scholes formula for valuing stock options except that the spot price of the underlying is replaced by the forward price F.

The Black formula for a European call option on an underlying strike at K, expiring T years in the future is

$$c = e^{-rT}[FN(d_1) - KN(d_2)]$$

    a. Multivariate normal distribution
    b. Black model
    c. Fama-French three factor model
    d. Moving average

17. In financial mathematics, _____ defines a relationship between the price of a call option and a put option--both with the identical strike price and expiry. To derive the _____ relationship, the assumption is that the options are not exercised before expiration day, which necessarily applies to European options. _____ can be derived in a manner that is largely model independent.

    a. Hull-White model
    b. Put-call parity
    c. Rendleman-Bartter model
    d. Cox-Ingersoll-Ross model

Chapter 21. Swaps: Economic Analysis and Pricing

18. In finance, the _____ between two currencies specifies how much one currency is worth in terms of the other. For example an _____ of 102 Japanese yen to the United States dollar means that JPY 102 is worth the same as USD 1. The foreign exchange market is one of the largest markets in the world.

a. ABN Amro
b. A Random Walk Down Wall Street
c. Exchange rate
d. AAB

19. In finance, the yield curve is the relation between the interest rate (or cost of borrowing) and the time to maturity of the debt for a given borrower in a given currency. For example, the current U.S. dollar interest rates paid on U.S. Treasury securities for various maturities are closely watched by many traders, and are commonly plotted on a graph such as the one on the right which is informally called 'the yield curve.' More formal mathematical descriptions of this relation are often called the _____.

The yield of a debt instrument is the annualized percentage increase in the value of the investment.

a. 7-Eleven
b. 4-4-5 Calendar
c. 529 plan
d. Term structure of interest rates

Chapter 22. Swaps: Applications

1. In finance, a _____ is a derivative in which two counterparties agree to exchange one stream of cash flows against another stream. These streams are called the legs of the _____.

   The cash flows are calculated over a notional principal amount, which is usually not exchanged between counterparties.

   a. Volatility arbitrage
   b. Local volatility
   c. Volatility swap
   d. Swap

2. _____ is that which is owed; usually referencing assets owed, but the term can cover other obligations. In the case of assets, _____ is a means of using future purchasing power in the present before a summation has been earned. Some companies and corporations use _____ as a part of their overall corporate finance strategy.

   a. Cross-collateralization
   b. Credit cycle
   c. Debt
   d. Partial Payment

3. A _____ is a fungible, negotiable instrument representing financial value. They are broadly categorized into debt securities (such as banknotes, bonds and debentures), and equity securities; e.g., common stocks. The company or other entity issuing the _____ is called the issuer.

   a. Tracking stock
   b. Securities lending
   c. Book entry
   d. Security

4. In finance, the _____ of a financial asset measures the sensitivity of the asset's price to interest rate movements, expressed as a number of years. The reason for expressing this sensitivity in years is that the time that will elapse until a cash flow is received allows more interest to accumulate. Therefore the price of an asset with long term cashflows has more interest rate sensitivity than an asset with cashflows in the near future.

   a. Macaulay duration
   b. Yield to maturity
   c. 4-4-5 Calendar
   d. Duration

5. _____ is a fee paid on borrowed assets. It is the price paid for the use of borrowed money, or, money earned by deposited funds. Assets that are sometimes lent with _____ include money, shares, consumer goods through hire purchase, major assets such as aircraft, and even entire factories in finance lease arrangements.

Chapter 22. Swaps: Applications

a. Insolvency
b. AAB
c. A Random Walk Down Wall Street
d. Interest

6. An _____ is the price a borrower pays for the use of money they do not own, and the return a lender receives for deferring the use of funds, by lending it to the borrower. _____s are normally expressed as a percentage rate over the period of one year.

_____s targets are also a vital tool of monetary policy and are used to control variables like investment, inflation, and unemployment.

a. ABN Amro
b. A Random Walk Down Wall Street
c. Interest rate
d. AAB

7. _____ is the risk (variability in value) borne by an interest-bearing asset, such as a loan or a bond, due to variability of interest rates. In general, as rates rise, the price of a fixed rate bond will fall, and vice versa. _____ is commonly measured by the bond's duration.

a. Interest rate risk
b. Official bank rate
c. A Random Walk Down Wall Street
d. International Fisher effect

8. In business and accounting, _____s are everything of value that is owned by a person or company. The balance sheet of a firm records the monetary value of the _____s owned by the firm. The two major _____ classes are tangible _____s and intangible _____s.

a. Asset
b. Accounts payable
c. Income
d. EBITDA

9. In the most general sense, a _____ is anything that is a hindrance, or puts individuals at a disadvantage. Before we discuss the financial terms, we should note that a _____ can also have a much more important slang meaning.

Chapter 22. Swaps: Applications

This is best described in an example.

a. Limited liability
b. Covenant
c. McFadden Act
d. Liability

10. The _____ is a financial and accounting term for the difference between the duration of assets and liabilities, and is typically used by banks, pension funds, or other financial institutions to measure their risk due to changes in the interest rate. This is one of the mismatches that can occur and are known as asset liability mismatches. Another way to define _____ is : it is the difference in the sensitivity of interest-yielding assets and the sensitivity of liabilities (of the organization) to a change in market interest rates (yields.)

a. Net worth
b. Modern portfolio theory
c. Debt cash flow
d. Duration gap

11. An _____ is a type of bond or other type of debt instrument used in finance whose coupon rate has an inverse relationship to short-term interest rates (or its reference rate.) With an _____, as interest rates rise the coupon rate falls. The basic structure is the same as an ordinary floating rate note except for the direction in which the coupon rate is adjusted.

a. A Random Walk Down Wall Street
b. AAB
c. ABN Amro
d. Inverse floater

12. _____ (or spoilage) refers to the process by which tissues of dead organisms break down into simpler forms of matter. Such a breakdown of dead organisms is essential for new growth and development of living organisms because it recycles the finite chemical constituents and frees up the limited physical space in the biome. Bodies of living organisms begin to decompose shortly after death.

a. 529 plan
b. 4-4-5 Calendar
c. Decomposition
d. 7-Eleven

13. A _____ is a type of derivative in which the underlying is denominated in one currency, but the instrument itself is settled in another currency at some fixed rate. Such products are attractive for speculators and investors who wish to have exposure to a foreign asset, but without the corresponding exchange rate risk.

Chapter 22. Swaps: Applications

Common types of _____ include :

- _____ futures contracts, such as a futures contract on a European stock market index which is settled in US dollars.
- _____ options, in which the difference between the underlying and a fixed strike price is paid out in another currency.
- _____ swaps, in which one counterparty pays a non-local interest rate to the other, but the notional amount is in local currency. The second party may be paying a fixed or floating rate. For example, a swap in which the notional amount is denominated in Canadian dollars, but where the floating rate is set as USD LIBOR, would be considered a _____ swap.

a. Volatility arbitrage
b. Dollar roll
c. Credit default swap index
d. Quanto

14. An _____ can be defined as a contract which provides an income stream in return for an initial payment. An immediate _____ is an _____ for which the time between the contract date and the date of the first payment is not longer than the time interval between payments. A common use for an immediate _____ is to provide a pension to a retired person or persons.

a. AT'T Inc.
b. Annuity
c. Intrinsic value
d. Amortization

15. An _____ is a swap where a set of future cash flows are exchanged between two counterparties. The two cash flows are usually referred to as 'legs'. One of these cash flow streams can be pegged to floating rate of interest or pay a fixed rate

a. Interest rate derivative
b. Interest rate swap
c. Equity swap
d. Interest rate future

Chapter 22. Swaps: Applications

16. A _____ rate loan is a loan where the interest rate doesn't fluctuate during the fixed rate period of the loan. This allows the borrower to accurately predict their future payments. Variable rate loans, by contrast, are anchored to the prevailing discount rate.

    a. Reference rate
    b. Fixed interest
    c. Cash accumulation equation
    d. SONIA

17. A _____ is an option granting its owner the right but not the obligation to enter into an underlying swap. Although options can be traded on a variety of swaps, the term '_____' typically refers to options on interest rate swaps.

    There are two types of _____ contracts:

    - A payer _____ gives the owner of the _____ the right to enter into a swap where they pay the fixed leg and receive the floating leg.
    - A receiver _____ gives the owner of the _____ the right to enter into a swap where they will receive the fixed leg, and pay the floating leg.

    The buyer and seller of the _____ agree on:

    - the premium (price) of the _____
    - the strike rate (equal to the fixed rate of the underlying swap)
    - length of the option period (which usually ends two business days prior to the start date of the underlying swap),
    - the term of the underlying swap,
    - notional amount,
    - amortization, if any
    - frequency of settlement of payments on the underlying swap

    The participants in the _____ market are predominantly large corporations, banks, financial institutions and hedge funds. End users such as corporations and banks typically use _____s to manage interest rate risk arising from their core business or from their financing arrangements.

    a. Swaption
    b. Put option
    c. Straddle
    d. Bear call spread

Chapter 22. Swaps: Applications

18. An _____ is a contract written by a seller that conveys to the buyer the right -- but not the obligation -- to buy (in the case of a call _____) or to sell (in the case of a put _____) a particular asset, such as a piece of property such as, among others, a futures contract. In return for granting the _____, the seller collects a payment (the premium) from the buyer.

For example, buying a call _____ provides the right to buy a specified quantity of a security at a set strike price at some time on or before expiration, while buying a put _____ provides the right to sell.

a. OPTION
b. Annuity
c. Amortization
d. AT'T Mobility LLC

ANSWER KEY

Chapter 1
1. d 2. a 3. c 4. d 5. c 6. d 7. d 8. b 9. d 10. a
11. d 12. a 13. d 14. d 15. d 16. a 17. d 18. c

Chapter 2
1. d 2. a 3. b 4. b 5. b 6. b 7. d 8. b 9. b 10. d
11. c 12. c 13. a 14. d 15. d 16. a 17. d 18. b 19. d 20. d
21. d

Chapter 3
1. d 2. b 3. d 4. b 5. a 6. a 7. c 8. d 9. b 10. c
11. a 12. d 13. a 14. d 15. a 16. c 17. a 18. b 19. d 20. a
21. b 22. d 23. c

Chapter 4
1. d 2. d 3. d 4. d 5. a 6. d 7. d 8. a 9. a 10. d
11. d 12. b

Chapter 5
1. b 2. c 3. c 4. d 5. d 6. d 7. d 8. b 9. a 10. b
11. a 12. c 13. b 14. d 15. b 16. d

Chapter 6
1. d 2. c 3. a 4. d 5. d 6. a 7. a 8. d 9. d 10. c
11. d 12. d 13. d 14. b 15. d

Chapter 7
1. b 2. c 3. c 4. d 5. c 6. b 7. d 8. a 9. d 10. c
11. d 12. a

Chapter 8
1. d 2. d 3. d 4. d 5. d 6. a 7. d 8. b 9. d 10. c
11. a 12. c

Chapter 9
1. d 2. c 3. a 4. b 5. a 6. a 7. b 8. d 9. b 10. a
11. a 12. d 13. d

Chapter 10
1. d 2. b 3. d 4. c 5. d 6. d 7. d 8. d 9. b 10. c
11. d 12. d 13. c 14. d 15. a 16. c

Chapter 11
1. d 2. c 3. a 4. d 5. d 6. b 7. b 8. d 9. d 10. d
11. b 12. a 13. b 14. d 15. d

ANSWER KEY

Chapter 12
1. c 2. d 3. b 4. d 5. c 6. d 7. c 8. d 9. c 10. b

Chapter 13
1. d 2. d 3. d 4. c 5. d 6. d 7. a 8. d 9. b 10. c
11. d 12. d 13. b 14. b

Chapter 14
1. d 2. b 3. a 4. b 5. c 6. a 7. c

Chapter 15
1. d 2. a 3. d 4. d

Chapter 16
1. b 2. d 3. d 4. d 5. a

Chapter 17
1. d 2. a 3. b 4. d 5. a 6. d 7. a 8. a 9. c 10. a
11. d 12. b

Chapter 18
1. a 2. b 3. d 4. d 5. d 6. d

Chapter 19
1. d 2. d 3. d 4. d 5. a 6. b 7. b 8. d 9. d 10. b
11. d 12. c 13. c 14. a 15. d 16. b 17. c 18. d 19. d 20. d
21. c 22. b 23. a 24. d 25. a

Chapter 20
1. d 2. d 3. a 4. a 5. b 6. d 7. d 8. d 9. b 10. d
11. a 12. b 13. c 14. b 15. c 16. b 17. a 18. c

Chapter 21
1. d 2. c 3. b 4. d 5. d 6. d 7. b 8. d 9. a 10. b
11. c 12. b 13. d 14. d 15. b 16. b 17. b 18. c 19. d

Chapter 22
1. d 2. c 3. d 4. d 5. d 6. c 7. a 8. a 9. d 10. d
11. d 12. c 13. d 14. b 15. c 16. b 17. a 18. a

www.ingramcontent.com/pod-product-compliance
Lightning Source LLC
Chambersburg PA
CBHW081845230426
43669CB00018B/2819